☆☆ THE ☆☆
FUNNIEST
COP
STORIES EVER

✮✩ THE ✩✮
FUNNIEST
COP
STORIES EVER

**SCOTT BAKER AND
TOM PHILBIN**

**Andrews McMeel
Publishing, LLC**

Kansas City

THE FUNNIEST COP STORIES EVER

06 07 08 09 10 RR2 10 9 8 7 6 5 4 3 2 1

ISBN-13: 978-0-7407-6075-4
ISBN-10: 0-7407-6075-0

Library of Congress Control Number: 2006923315

www.andrewsmcmeel.com

ATTENTION: SCHOOLS AND BUSINESSES
Andrews McMeel books are available at quantity discounts with bulk purchase for educational, business, or sales promotional use. For information, please write to: Special Sales Department, Andrews McMeel Publishing, LLC, 4520 Main Street, Kansas City, Missouri 64111.

Thanks to Scott, a warm, sensitive, caring guy who also happens to be very funny, a great storyteller. I will always cherish those Sundays in Borders as we brought this wonderful (I think it is!) book to life and tittered, cackled, and howled and drank coffee that I always manipulated you into paying for.

Much thanks to Dina for getting us together, and thanks to Chris Schillig for her sensitive and insightful editing of the book.

Finally, thanks to "Brokejaw," one of the people in this book. Existence of guys like you makes books like this possible.

—*Tom Philbin*

To my father, who was the most dynamic storyteller I ever knew. To my mother, who always encouraged my humor. Also to my good friend, Justin Doyle: I should have been there for you more than I was; thank you for your forgiveness.

—*Scott Baker*

ACKNOWLEDGMENTS

☆

I would like to thank my dear friend Dina Masella-Frechen. Without her belief in me and her introduction to my coauthor, Tom Philbin, none of this would have been possible. While we are on the subject, I would also like to thank Tom Philbin, who was so much more than a coauthor to me on this project. He has been a true friend—I only wish I could have met him earlier in my life. I truly enjoyed getting together to discuss these stories with him and being forced to buy him his coffee; I will miss it. I would also like to give a very sincere thanks to my publisher, Andrews McMeel, and my editor, Christine Schillig. You took a chance on me and believed in this project, and I thank you from the bottom of my heart. Most of all I would like to thank all the police officers I have worked with, Ed Polstein and the NYPD Rant, and all the officers from all over the country who have contributed stories to this book. I had so much fun reliving some of these tales and appreciate you sharing them with me. It is special people like you that have the strength to find humor while putting your own lives on the line and protecting the lives of others. Thank you all.

Scott Baker

INTRODUCTION

When I was a cop with the NYPD, I saw so many funny things happen on the street that I thought that one day I would collect and write them in a book. This is the final result. For several years I went around interviewing cops from all over the country, and I found that the stories in Baltimore, LA, and everywhere else were as funny as any in New York. Nothing quite prepares you for what you see on the street once you become a cop. It is one of the most dangerous jobs, but also the most fun as well. One minute you are shot at; the next you are convincing a woman that there are no people from outer space after her. In what other profession will you find yourself chasing a midget in a tuxedo down a fire escape? Cops meet some of the zaniest, wildest, craziest characters that ever walked the face of the earth. The things a cop sees in his career could not be made up by the most creative Hollywood writers. Add to that the fact that these grown men have the mentality of college frat brothers and you have some of the funniest stories that ever happened. One cop described it as "going to high school with legal guns."

These stories are all true, and told in their own words with some editing by the cops who experienced them or heard them from other cops and retold them.

Cops are notoriously private people except when they're talking to other cops—the brotherhood of blue is strong—so I quickly assured them that no real names would be used and that no specific information would be provided that would allow even the most dogged investigator to determine who was telling the stories. Though funny, the unauthorized actions that cops took in some of these incidents might jeopardize their jobs. Ordinary cops love to laugh—it vents the pressure they're constantly under—but in general the brass approaches cop work with a stern and rigid interpretation of what a cop can or can't do. They often turn molehills into mountains in determining a cop's fate. Because the cops knew that they could not be identified, they spoke freely with no holds barred, and that led them to tell some very funny stories.

The enormous stress of a cop's job results in very unfunny 50 percent divorce and alcoholism rates. Many have developed a taste, as it were, for salty language— blue language, if you will. Most of that has been edited out because some people find it offensive, but excising curse words or obscenities doesn't affect the humor of the stories. In some cases the word [bleep] or [bleeping] has been substituted for curses because they are an integral part of the story; to use bland language would dilute the effect.

INTRODUCTION

The stories have a single goal: to make readers titter, cackle, howl, and chortle as well as laugh their [bleeps] off. And believe me, you will. I hope you enjoy reading them as much as I enjoyed living them and collecting them. Remember, the stories are all true. Only the names have been changed to protect the insane.

—Scott Baker

MR. ROSENTHAL'S REGRET

My partner and I go to an aided case (a person in need of medical assistance) on the north side of the expressway where a very old man is sitting in a lawn chair. He looks pale and weak. There are a few neighbors around, so I talk with one lady. "What's the problem?"

She tells me it's a very sad story. His name is Norman Rosenthal, and his wife passed away six or seven months ago. He's got diabetes and doesn't take care of himself, and every once in a while he passes out. That's what he did today. So they helped him into the lawn chair and called us.

So I go up to him and say, "What's the matter, Mr. Rosenthal?"

He answers in a thick Jewish accent, "Ah, I'm fine. Don't worry about me. Leave me alone already."

"Mr. Rosenthal, we called the paramedics and they're going to come here and check you out a little. But can I ask you something, did you eat today?"

"Don't worry about me. I don't need nothing to eat. I can take care of myself."

"Well, obviously not, Mr. Rosenthal. I heard you have diabetes, and when you don't eat, your blood sugar level is going to drop and you're going to pass out. So I want you to sit tight until the paramedics come and check you out. Meanwhile, I'm going across the street to the deli and get you something to eat so you'll have something in your system—"

"I don't need anything from the deli. I can take care of myself. I don't want to eat. I don't need anything."

My partner keeps his eye on the old guy while I go and get him a roll and butter. When I get back, I say: "Listen, Mr. Rosenthal. You got to eat something."

"I don't want to eat! Leave me alone! I'm not hungry!"

"Just take this," I said.

"All right!" He takes the roll and butter, looks up at me, and says, "What's the matter? You couldn't get me a sandwich?"

Ever Hear of a Door?

*M*e and my partner are driving down one of the streets
adjacent to McArthur Park one day and we see this tall,
skinny black guy walking down the block with a TV on
his shoulder. He's got a big Afro, but the strange thing is
that he appears to be a young guy but his hair looks white.
When we get closer we see it's some sort of powder, and
his clothing has white powder on it too.

We stop and ask him where he's going with the TV and
where he got it, but his answers are evasive. So we bore in
on him, and he finally admits that he stole the TV.

"Where from?" I ask him.

"I'll show you."

We load him in the car with the TV and he directs us
to a private house a few blocks away. He gives us a tour.
He explains that he noted that the windows and doors
were alarmed, so he had to go in another way. "Through
the back," he says.

We accompany him to the back of the house and there
in the middle of the wall is a big hole maybe two feet wide

3

and three feet high leading into what looks like the living room. What he did was remove shingles, sheathing, and plasterboard—the reason he was covered with white dust—and went through the wall. When he said he went through the back, he really meant it.

MOVING BODY

One day I was on a four-to-twelve tour in the Seven-Five precinct. It was February, cold as hell, and me and my partner, Danny, were nearing the end of our shift when we get a call from Central that there's a body lying on the sidewalk on Van Sinderan Avenue, in a deserted, factory area.

So we proceed over there and find this middle-aged guy lying facedown on the sidewalk. He's frozen solid. He is wearing tattered clothing, his face has a scruffy look, and there is a shopping cart full of crap nearby. He is obviously a homeless person. There is no blood, no sign of violence. He just dropped dead.

It is now about 11:15, so we figure that if things go the way they usually do, we'll have to safeguard the scene and stay until the ME finishes his examination. We'll be there for hours.

Now the Seven-Five is separated in parts from the Seven-Three just by Van Sinderan Avenue. We get an idea. We look around. No one is in sight. So Danny grabs

5

the arms, I grab the legs, and we pick up and carry the body across Van Sinderan and place it on the sidewalk. Then we call Central and say that we responded, but the case was unfounded—no complainant. Central says okay, and we drive to the precinct, turn in our radios, and go home.

The next night we do another four-to-twelve and we get a call for the same area as the night before. We ride by, and sure enough, the body is back on the Seven-Five Side. Turns out the Seven-Three guys had the same idea as us! This time we waited for the ME. Who knew where it might have ended if we didn't?

CALL A MECHANIC

I was walking a foot post in the Six-Eight, and I see some lady is on the street clutching her chest. I drop down and start CPR and a crowd gathers. I call a bus [ambulance], and as I'm working on her, some middle-aged mafioso wearing a sweat suit and a gold chain comes out of a storefront club and says, "What's going on!?"

Then a kid who looks like he should be on *Growin' Up Gotti* answers the question in a thick wannabe accent. "Yo, this lady's in Cadillac arrest!"

I have to keep working on her, but I'm dying inside trying not to laugh as this woman is struggling to hold on to life. Finally, the bus comes and she ends up being okay. But as I'm getting in the bus to go to the hospital to fill out the forms, I can't help being a wise guy to the kid.

"Hey! Doogie Howser, M.D. Thanks for the help."

"Yo, no problem."

EYEWITNESS

☆

This drunken Spanish guy robbed a woman on Crestview Road. We caught him, and usually when we do this we have what is called a "showup," where the complainant tries to ID the suspect at the scene of the crime. If you bring the suspect to the complainant when he's already in cuffs and in the police car, it can skew the complainant's judgment. They might automatically think that the guy is guilty and ID him. Of course, it's not perfect, but a showup works.

Anyway, they bring the lady to the suspect, who is still drunk. When he sees her pull up he looks at her and says, *"Sí, that's the one I rob."*

The Violin Should Help

*M*e and my partner, Nicky, get a call to go to a building on Church Street. A woman is calling for help, that she's been assaulted. So we go to the building and the woman is leaning out a fifth-story window yelling, "Up here! Up here!"

We go running up the stairs, and when we get there, we see that the old wooden door has been knocked in—it's hanging on by a single hinge. Inside we find a heavyset, thirtyish Spanish woman. She's very upset and she's got a shiner. We ask her what happened.

"My boyfriend," she says. "He beat me up, then ran up the fire escape."

So we get on the radio and talk to Central and confirm a woman has been assaulted, and they should stand by for a description of the suspect. Then we ask the woman what the boyfriend looks like. "How big is he?"

"He's short, a little short."

"How short, approximately?"

"Well, he's less than four feet. Three feet ten inches. He's a midget."

9

Both of us are trying to hold our laughter in, and we're looking at the door and wondering how a midget could kick it in, and Nicky says, "How was he able to kick in the door?"

"He's a karate expert."

Somehow, Nicky is able to speak into the radio and he says, "Central, be advised that the suspect is three feet, ten inches, and is a midget, Hispanic, and he was last seen fleeing up the fire escape of the building."

Then voices start coming back over the radio from other units who are going to canvass the area. One guy says, "Well, is he a midget or a dwarf?"

Nicky asks why it matters, and somebody says, "A midget has a small head that is in proportion to his body while a dwarf has a small body but a big head."

Nicky asks the lady, "Is he a midget or a dwarf?"

"He's a midget."

"Central, be advised he's definitely a midget. Stand by for a description of what the suspect was wearing." One of us asks the lady, "Ma'am, what was he wearing?"

"Well, he was wearing a tuxedo and carrying a violin case. He was going to propose to me."

Me and Nicky are dying, but Nicky manages to say into the radio. "He's three feet, ten inches, wearing a tuxedo, and carrying a violin case."

Central says okay and we get on the fire escape. Just as we reach the roof some rookie comes on the radio and says, "Central. What does the suspect actually look like? Do you have a physical description?"

Nicky gets a strange look in his eyes and gets on the radio. "Dude," he said, "do me a favor! Stop any [bleeping] midget wearing a tux and carrying a violin case. Who the [bleep] cares what he [bleeping] looks like!"

OLICE LINE - DO NOT CROSS   POLICE LINE - DO NO

A NEW PERSON

About five years ago, I was in the robbery squad, and me and Detective Eddie Weeks made a robbery collar one Saturday night about midnight. It was a basic robbery, nothing special. The suspect was a Chinese guy. We take him back to the station, photograph him, and the guy gives us his pedigree information, including the fact that his name is David Wu. Eddie checks him out on the computer, gets no warrants, no hits.

The next morning, our boss, Sergeant Costa, comes in and says, "What happened last night?"

"Nothing," I said, "just a robbery collar."

"Let me see the information."

So we give him the file and he starts thumbing through it and sees Wu's photo and says, "This isn't David Wu, this is David Gong."

Eddie says, "David Gong? This is David Wu. Who's David Gong?" But we both realize that in the Chinese culture people change names like they change socks.

"He's wanted in the One-Twelve," Costa says, "for the murder of a livery cab driver."

"Maybe," Weeks says, "they just look alike."

"No, listen," Costa says, "I'm very familiar with him. I talked with him before—locked him up. I'm telling you this is David Gong. Where is he?"

"In the interrogation room."

As soon as we walk in, this guy David Wu knows exactly who Costa is. So Costa says, "Hey David, how you doin'?"

"Hey Sarge, how are you?"

"So when did you change your name?"

"Last night when I got arrested."

AND ONE COUNT
OF STUPIDITY

☆

This guy Pat Colon tells me that he once collared this huge, muscle-bound guy on a robbery charge. The only problem is that this guy is mute, a statue. "I couldn't get him to say anything," Colon said, "no matter what I said. So finally I said to him that I was just going to book him on robbery two and that was that. Then he comes alive. His brow wrinkles with concern and his eyes widen, and he says, 'Robbery two? I just rob one person!'"

A NASTY PRANK

One night around one in the morning, me and my partner, Jay, were in an unmarked car and we observed this black woman walking along. A couple of cars slowed down and stopped next to her. Whoever was inside exchanged conversation with the woman and then took off. But then a third car came along, a white Cadillac. It stopped, and after a conversation with the driver, the woman got in the car, which was the whole criteria for soliciting prostitution. So we stopped the car and arrested the woman.

On the way back to the station we search through her purse and find a driver's license for a man plus credit cards in the same name. The collar is looking better. We may get her for a CPSP [Criminal Possession of Stolen Property], or pop her on a robbery warrant. I ask her, "Where'd you get the ID and credit cards?"

"They're mine."

"What?"

"I'm a man. I'm taking hormone shots, and I'm going to get the operation."

Me and Jay are stunned. It's unbelievable. This guy looks as good as any girl. Nice body, pretty, long wig, nice skin, the works. It occurs to me that me and Jay were not the only ones fooled. Think of all the guys that ended up being propositioned by this guy.

Anyway, we take him back to the station, and everyone else is marveling that this girl is a man. Then Jay has an idea. "Let's play a little prank on someone based on how incredible the guy looks, see if we can fool them. But who?"

"How about Joanne Alana?" someone suggests.

There is immediate agreement. Joanne is a plainclothes cop, smart, knowledgeable, and tough —a great cop—but she can also take a joke.

So Joanne is radioed by the desk sergeant and he asks her to come to the house, that we have a pros [prostitute] in custody and would you mind giving her a good toss? [Male cops can't thoroughly search female suspects.] Being the good team player she is, Joanne says no problem, but there is one stipulation. "Is she clean?" Joanne asks. "I am not touching any more AIDS-infected crack whores."

"Sure," the desk sergeant says. "She's clean. You know you can trust us."

Joanne's mind must have been on vacation, because she believed him. When a cop says "Trust me," it's time to leave. So she comes in and takes the pros into a female bathroom and everyone goes to the door and listens. Joanne starts frisking him, saying various things and then she says, "What's this?"

"That's my tampon."

"It's too big to be a tampon. Lift your skirt and drop your panties."

Then Joanne yells, "Holy [bleep]!" and she comes storming out the door. Her face is red as a beet. "I'm going to kill you [bleeping] guys!"

Everyone was hysterical laughing when Jay says with a straight face, "Listen, you just said you didn't want to toss an AIDS-infected crack whore. You said nothing about an AIDS-infected, cross-dressing, pre-op, transsexual crack whore!"

Fair Is Fair

You deal with all kinds of mentals on the job, but the one I remember most occurred before cell phones near the bus station on Main Street. A person was harassing people who were lined up waiting to use a pay phone. From the description—he's a big bushy-haired guy with a gray beard wearing old Army clothes—I know I've dealt with him before. He's mental and mean, from Creighton Mental Hospital a short way away. I knew him from his harassment of people at the railroad station. He would ask for money, and if they didn't give it to him, he would throw down his pants and defecate.

What he was doing now was asking the person who was on the phone for spare change. If the person said "No," he would hang up their phone. When they reached into their pockets to take out more change he would yell in their face, "I thought you didn't have any change?" Then he would interfere with them making another call. Fortunately, we were able to get him to leave without a problem. Every time I think of him, I think that when you're crazy you have cojones the size of Kansas.

A GOOD SCARE

☆

I used to work in Crown Heights. It's half Haitian and half Hasidic, and the Jews are a big voting bloc because they all vote together. They had connections in the department, and if you pissed the wrong guy off you could be sure that by the time you got back to the precinct, there would be a phone call waiting for you. Somebody high up would want to know why you gave such-and-such a ticket.

An old-time cop named Johnny Grant really got fed up with this, just sick and tired of dealing with all the political B.S. So one day this Hasid commits a traffic violation and Johnny stops him. Now most people have different ways to ask a cop not to give them the ticket, like, "Give me a break," "I was distracted," "I was on my way to see my dying mother," et cetera. But the Hasidim had their own way of asking, and it was invariably the same. The Hasid said it to Johnny on this occasion, "Please officer, don't give me a ticket. Just give me a good scare." So Johnny went back to his car and a few minutes later goes back to the Hasid, hands him a ticket, and says, "Boo."

HOW NOT TO MAKE A NEW FRIEND

Back in 1992, when I was in the 109, the brass really cracked down on cops because of Michael Dowd, a dirty cop whose activities cast suspicion on everyone. One of the crackdowns involved the Interrupted Patrol Log. If you came off patrol for any reason, you were required to go to the desk sergeant, sign in, and state why you were in the precinct. They wanted to keep close track of everyone.

So one day I came in to the precinct to voucher a stolen vehicle, and I passed the desk and the sergeant on duty. This guy had just transferred over from another precinct, and I didn't know him, so he looks at my nametag and says, "Baker, did you sign the Interrupted Patrol Log?"

I didn't know what to make of his question, because he had winked as he asked it, and I didn't know if he was serious. But I decided to play along, and said, "Sure," and winked back and went about my business. I figured it was okay because he was an old timer and agreed with other old timers about what crap these crackdowns were.

Five or ten minutes later my business brought me past the desk again, and again he stopped me. "Baker, did you sign the log yet?" Again, he winked, this time a couple of times. I still didn't know what to do, so again I played along, winked back a couple of times, and went away.

Maybe ten minutes later I go past the desk again. This time, Sergeant stops me and says really seriously, "Did you sign the freakin' log?"

But now he was winking like three or four times. "Sure," I said, winking back.

He picks up the log and says: "Where?"

As he's saying this he's still winking. I don't know what the hell is going on. But I wink back and sign the log.

A few days later I was talking with some other cops and I tell them what happened. One of them knew the sergeant from the Four-Six, and he smiled broadly. "Hey you idiot! He wasn't winking. He's got a facial tic!"

GUESSING GAME

I was on patrol on Bay Street where there are always livery cabs—most of them illegal. Today it had snowed heavily, and the snow was piled up along the curbs. Openings had been shoveled in the piles so people could get to the buses that stopped there, but some of the cabs were parking right next to the openings, making people climb over the snow to get to the buses.

We'd tell the drivers to move along, and usually they'd do it. There was this one Indian guy who wouldn't move. So on Monday I gave him a ticket. Tuesday when he did it again I gave him another ticket, and also on Wednesday. I start to write another ticket for Thursday and he says to me in a heavy Indian accent, "Officer Leary, this is not fair. Monday you give me ticket, Tuesday you give me ticket, Wednesday you give me ticket, and today you give me ticket. Every day you give me ticket—"

"Well, every day you park at a bus stop, you'll get one. It's not like you're immune for the rest of the month if I give you one at the beginning of the month. Every day you park illegally I'm going to give you another ticket."

"No, very unfair! Very unfair. Don't give me ticket every day."

"Hey, don't tell me what I'm allowed to do."

"I want your badge number!"

So I cover the badge on my chest with my hand and say, "You can't have it."

"I want it!"

"No, you can't. You can only have the one on my cap. You can't have the one on my chest." Of course the badge on my chest and the cap are the same.

"No, I don't want the one on the cap!"

"Okay, I'll tell you what I'll do. I'll take my hand away for three seconds. If you can get it you can have it." So I start playing peek-a-boo with my hand on and off the badge, but he can't get the number, and he's pissed.

Anyway, he goes to the precinct and tells the desk sergeant about how I'm giving him a ticket every day, and I won't give him my badge number—only the one on the cap.

When I come in, the sergeant calls me over and tells me the guy came in to make a complaint.

He says, "Do me a favor, knock it off out there. I got better things to do with my time than mess around with this jerk."

I held my hand over my nameplate and said, "How do you know it was me?"

"Donde Es el Pollo?"

*O*ne spring evening, me and my partner, Eddie, walk into a bodega on East Tremont Avenue because Eddie's got to take a leak pretty bad. The bodega is sort of typical—deli case and counter in front, narrow aisles with shelves with food on them. A Hispanic man and woman are behind the counter, and there are a couple of young kids running up and down the aisles. So Eddie says to the man and woman, *"Buenos dias, señor and señorita. Como estás?"*

"Bueno, bueno."

"Bueno."

He says another few things, and I know he's showing off his Spanish.

Then he asks where the bathroom is in Spanish, but instead of saying *"Donde es el baño?"* he says, *"Donde es el pollo?"* which means "Where is the chicken?"

The people look at him blankly. They don't know what he's talking about, but I do. I say nothing. I'm just trying to hold in my laughter, which is enhanced because I know he's got to go. He repeats himself. *"Donde es el pollo?"*

The guy puts out his hands, shakes his head a little and says, *"No tengo pollo,"* meaning, "I have no chicken."

Then I see Eddie sneakily touch his crotch and give it a squeeze. He really has to go bad. It's taking me everything I got to hold my laughter in. "I have to use the *pollo*!" he says more urgently. Of course, he's saying, "I got to use the chicken!"

Now I see that the kids, who were likely educated in America, are laughing hysterically—because they know what he's saying, and it's rare to see a cop grabbing his crotch. "C'mon," Eddie says, his face a little white, legs moving. "You want me to pee on the counter? I got to use the *pollo*."

"Señor," the guy says, "you're asking to pee on the chicken."

I burst out laughing, and Eddie says, "Oh! Do you have a bathroom I can use?"

"Yes." The man points. "In the back of the store."

Eddie scuttled away, holding his crotch. I hate to say it, but it was a pisser.

POLICE LINE - DO NOT CROSS   POLICE LINE - DO NO

AN UNFAMILIAR PLACE

Me and my partner, Jimmy Antonelli, go to a domestic dispute at an apartment and see two people who could not be more opposite in appearance. The woman stands about four-two, four-three, short and built like an ash can. The man is six feet, very thin, has a drawn look like you see in a health-food store. Neither of them is very attractive, and he has this whiny, nasal voice and talked very slowly. "Officers, I'm so, so glad you're here."

Now there's no physical violence, apparently they were just arguing. So Jimmy asks, "What's the problem?"

"Officer," the guy says in that whiny voice, "she's crazy. A lunatic. She's gone off her rocker. I can't get hold of her doctor. Look what she did."

I look at the woman. She's not saying a word. "What'd she do?" I ask.

He points to a table on which there are nine or ten bottles of medication—without the labels. "She tore the labels off. She doesn't know what medication to take."

"Well," I said, "can you call the doctor?"

"I don't have the number," he whines, "it was on the labels. I was looking in information. I can't find it!"

I say, "Ma'am, did you do this?"

She answers loud and fast like a machine gun. "That's right! I did it! I did it. And you know why? Because I want him out! I want someone else. Anyone! Anyone! Anyone but him. Anyone! Out!" She keeps repeating it over and over again. Then, very abruptly, she stops. He says, "See what I'm putting up with? She's crazy. She's a lunatic. She's nuts."

Then she starts again, a mile a minute, "I want him out of here! Out of here! Out of here!"

"Officer," he said, "I love her, but look at the abuse I take! I mean is it so wrong to want to make love with your wife?"

In my mind I'm looking at her and thinking, With her—yes. Anyway, I tell him that I can't keep coming back here, and I can't institutionalize her because she's not doing anything violent. She obviously doesn't want the guy in the house, and we can't force him to leave, but I would suggest he either get in touch with the doctor to medicate her or stay somewhere else for the night and get in touch with the doctor in the morning. "Is there any place you can go?"

"I guess I can go to my sister's." Then he looks at the woman and says very sweetly, "Honey, do you have the spare key?"

"Yeah," she says rapid fire, "yeah. It's right here in my panties!"

His eyes roll back, and he's says, "Oh my God! I'll never get it! I haven't been down there in years!"

INCINERATED

☆

When someone is arrested, they have a choice of holding on to certain items of their property or getting it vouchered [held by the police department] and returned to them when they're released. It's definitely safer to have it vouchered. When you go through the system there's a good chance you'll lose it or have it stolen.

Onc timc, I'm on the desk, and this guy who had vouchered his property with us called. "I want to get my property back. I was incinerated there last night."

"Oh," I said, "you might want to call the fire department."

"No man! You guys incinerated me!"

"So, didn't you go to the hospital?"

"For what?"

"Burns."

"What burns? Man, I was incinerated there."

"You mean you were incarcerated."

"Oh, call it what you want. I just want my property back."

A BRAVE THIEF

New York City is famous for three things: its people, its culture, and its rats.

The rats are huge, and there are tons of them. So one day, me and the sergeant who's riding with me get a call to go to a possible burglary in a Chinese bakery in a dirty party of town. We get there, and my sergeant tells me to search the basement. With gun drawn, I make my way down the concrete stairs, and the light is very dim. As soon as I step on the basement floor, a rat the size of a small baby runs across my shoe, and I freeze. I know if there's one rat, he ain't alone. I think about going deeper into the cellar, which is really dark, and there's no light switch in sight. So I go back upstairs, and the sergeant asks, "Anyone down there?"

"No, it's clear," I say, thinking, except for the rat convention, and I figure if the burglar is down there, my hat's off to him. He deserves every penny he robs.

A Sad Story

I was working the Halloween Parade in Greenwich Village with my partner Mike McCabe. It's a famous event, and a lot of gay people take part in it. The parade has already started, and we're just there shooting the breeze. All of a sudden, this thin, pretty, small gay guy comes running down the street. He's wearing lingerie, heavy makeup, and a feather boa. He says with a very pronounced lisp, "Excuse me, Officer! Excuse me—where's the parade?"

So I tell him just go down Houston. "You can't miss it."

"Thank you so much." He takes about five steps, whirls around, looks at Mike, bats his eyes, and says, "You, you're so handsome. I could spend a lifetime with you!" Then he looks at me, "But you, you have bedroom eyes, so you're just a one-night stand."

He turns and goes away, and I say to McCabe, my face sad, "How come no one can ever commit to me? I feel like just a piece of meat!"

31

LOST HIS WAY

The 111 in Queens borders the Nassau County Police Department, and sometimes it's confusing as to whose jurisdiction a case is, the city's or the county's. So cops from both usually went out on calls and sorted out whose collar it was later.

This one time, we go out there and arrest a guy for a burglary at a house straddling the county line. We arrest him and put him in the back of the car, and he figures he has no problem because he knows at that time, the city was a revolving door of justice. You go in front of a judge, and he says, "You caught him, nobody got hurt. Okay, six months."

Then the Nassau cops show up at the scene. Our sergeant and the Nassau sergeant talk it over. Turns out the guy broke into the house on the Nassau side of the county line. So we have to hand him over, and they didn't treat burglary like we did. They treated it very seriously. So we get the guy out of our patrol car, and he asks, "What you doing?"

We explain that he broke into the house on the Nassau side, and we're handing him over. "Oh no," he says, "no, no, no! I broke in on the city side!" He is panicking, because he knows he's going to do about three years. You can't burglarize houses in Nassau like the city. There's civilization there.

"City side! City side! City side. Going to the city jail, not the Nassau jail!"

Now the guy starts fighting with us. He's nasty, spitting, cursing. He even gets a little bloodied up in the struggle. As he was being put in the Nassau patrol car, my partner says, "Next time instead of burglar tools bring a [bleeping] map!"

ALIVE WORKS
BETTER

When you're in the academy, they teach you that if you go to a crime scene or an auto accident and there are body parts, you're supposed to pick up the part, pack it in ice, and get it to the hospital. They may be able to sew it back on or whatever.

So there is an accident where a guy was decapitated, and the first cop on the scene packed his head in ice. When I arrive I say to the cop, "What the hell are you going to do with that?"

"In the academy they tell us to pack parts in ice."

"Yeah! You jackass. But a living limb, an arm, a finger that can be reattached, not a head!"

WE MARRIED, BUT . . .

Me and Mike Talmone were in the section of the precinct where the abandoned buildings are. It's a bad area where all the prostitutes go, a lot of crack is sold, and every once in a while you get a shooting. It's a place where dealers go to test their guns. It's like a perp shooting range—you see the street signs with bullet holes in them.

Anyway, we're on a four-to-twelve, and we see a car parked with its windows all fogged up and movement in the back. We don't know what's going on, whether someone's being raped or doing drugs—it's all happened in this area before. So we pull up nose to nose to the car with our lights, and the searchlight is on, so whoever's in there will know we're cops, not some perverts.

We can see inside, and we see a couple of people, looks like a man and a woman, scurrying to get their clothes on. We tell them to get out, and they do. It's two Chinese people, a man and a woman, maybe in their mid-thirties. We have to question them, because we still don't know what's going on. Might be a rape. So Talmone takes the woman aside to talk with her, and I take the man. I say to the guy, "What's the story? What you doing back there?"

"Oh, uh, we together back here."

I think he's trying to show me he doesn't speak English at all so I say, "I understand, you're doing chop chop. But you can't do chop chop here. You married?"

"Yeah," he says, "we married."

I nod and say, "Okay. It's dangerous. Shouldn't be taking your wife back here to do chop chop. People get raped and robbed here. Go home. If the kids are home, go to a motel, spring for a couple of dollars."

He nods, and I go around to where Mike is talking with the woman and I say to him, "They're married."

Talmone shakes his head, "They're not married. They work together. She just told me the whole story. They just work in the same office."

So I go back to the guy and say, "I thought you said you were married?"

"We married," he says, "but not to each other."

By the Book

Years ago there used to be a unit called FIAU, Field Internal Affairs Unit. The guys weren't even internal affairs guys—they were inspections guys. They didn't want to go on the street; they didn't want to do real police work. Their sole purpose was to try and screw cops, and they didn't go after cops who were doing anything really illegal—just cops doing little stuff, minor infractions. Like if they caught you on patrol with white socks, they'd write you up. You'd get what they call a CD, a Command Discipline, or a "rip." You could lose a vacation day just for that.

They gave my partner, Bert, a rip for a "bent cap device." The shield on the top of the cap was bent because Bert was chasing a guy, and his hat fell off onto the street and bent the little Indian on the top. But you couldn't explain that to this hump. Bert got written up.

Two weeks later, he is standing at the newsstand right above the subway on a hot, sweltering day, and he buys a newspaper, which is an infraction. You can't buy one, have one, or read one while you're on patrol. As soon as he buys the newspaper, he sees the sergeant from FIAU—the same one who had given him a rip two weeks earlier—coming down the block. He doesn't know if the sergeant saw him buy the newspaper or not, but he knows he could get another rip. He thinks fast and yells to the sergeant, "Sarge! Follow me!"

He knows the guy doesn't want to get involved, but he's required to. The sergeant starts running, and when he's close, Bert yells again, "Follow me! Follow me!"

"What's the matter?"

Bert doesn't answer, but he runs down the subway steps, the sergeant behind him. The subway is even hotter than the street, like the inside of an oven, and this sergeant is not in uniform—he's got a suit on, so it's even hotter.

They run and run and run. Bert takes him at top speed all the way to the end of the platform, and the FIAU guy was really out of shape. By the time they get to the end of the platform, the guy is sweating freely, his head looks like a tomato, and he's out of breath. Then Bert turns and says, "Ah [bleep]! The guy was [bleeping] me!"

"What do you mean?"

"A guy told me that there was a pregnant woman giving birth down here on the platform, and in the academy they teach you to catch the baby in a newspaper."

POLICE LINE - DO NOT CROSS   POLICE LINE - DO NOT

The sergeant didn't believe him for a second. "You turd! You made me run the length of this platform in a hundred and three–degree weather just to avoid another rip?"

But Bert stuck by his story. "No, no," he says, "a passerby told me. A passerby told me, and you know we have to do things by the book."

OLICE LINE – DO NOT CROSS   POLICE LINE – DO NO

BE A LITTLE PATIENT

When you go into the psycho ward at Bellevue with an EDP [emotionally disturbed person], the procedure is usually to bring him to a waiting room and sit there with him until a doctor can see him and tell you whether he can go home or they're going to keep him for observation. The hospital takes people from all over the city, so you're usually sitting there with other cops and their EDPs and maybe a hospital cop.

Anyway, one time I'm sitting in the psycho ward, and another cop's EDP starts having an episode. He runs around yelling, "I'm shrinking! I'm shrinking! I'm shrinking! Help me!" He does this for about five minutes, and finally I yell out, "Hey, calm down! You just have to be a little patient! Get it?"

He obviously didn't get it, but the other cops did and they were roaring.

VERY IMPORTANT
TO KNOW

We got an aided call to a bodega in Spanish Harlem where a woman is having a seizure or something. So me and my partner rush in and ask this middle-aged Hispanic guy, "Are you the proprietor?"

"No. I don't know who that is. I'm the owner." Then he takes us back to the woman, who's lying on her back in an aisle and twitching a bit. My partner says to the owner, "Is she epileptic?"

"I don't know. I think she's a Methodist."

THE RECEIPT

We got a call to go to the 103 to help them quell civil unrest in a shopping center. This center was overrun with wolf packs—kids from a local high school who would band together in groups of a dozen or more, invade stores, and take what they wanted. The owners couldn't stop them. Our goal was to create a police presence that would scare the kids away.

Because we were from the Bronx, our radios didn't work in the 103—we're on different frequencies. So when we got there, radios were issued to our sergeants so they could stay in touch with the cops from the 103.

We set up and stay for twelve hours, and the kids get the message. They don't come into the center. At the end of the day, we pile into our van to head back to the Bronx, but Sergeant Decker tells one of the cops named Shalimo that he forgot to return the radio to the mobile command unit, and Shalimo should run it back. Then he adds, "And don't forget a receipt."

Now Shalimo is a very experienced cop, and when Decker tells him to get a receipt, Shalimo thinks it's a joke because he never heard of such [bleep]. But he leaves with the radio. From Decker's point of view, it was not a bunch of bull. If you lose a radio, they will launch a major investigation. They don't want some perp directing cops to go into one area of a precinct when he's robbing another.

Shalimo comes back, gets in the van, and Decker starts driving. We go a little ways, and Decker says, "Where is it?"

"I got it."

"Let me have it."

Decker continues to drive, and when Shalimo doesn't give him the receipt he barks out, "Where's the [bleeping] receipt? Give it to me now!"

Shalimo nods, then takes out a piece of paper and hands it to Decker. He reads it and then growls, "What the [bleep] is this?"

"The receipt."

Decker's really annoyed. He stops the van and says to Shalimo, "Go back and get a [bleeping] receipt!"

Shalimo goes back and gets one. Later we learned that he had written on the paper he handed Decker, "I owe you one radio."

ONE OLD COP

☆

There was this guy," said one detective, "named Larry Kennedy. He was the oldest cop I ever met on the job. He had to have at least forty years in, maybe more."

"How old was he?"

"I don't know exactly," the detective replied, "but I do know that when the Indians came into the precinct to file a complaint that the white man had stolen Manhattan, he was the one who took it."

The Secret Sauce

*C*ops have all kinds of mental cases come up to them on the street, but you have to take every complaint seriously until you understand what's really going on. Me and my partner were on foot patrol when a middle-aged female comes running up to us. Her eyes are on fire.

"I want to make a complaint," she says, "about McDonald's."

"What's the matter?" I ask.

"They won't hire me."

"Do you think it's racial?" I say.

"I don't know. But they won't hire me. I been there ten times in six months. I want to work there!"

My partner says very seriously, "Well, maybe they think you'll steal the secret sauce."

Her face screws up, "What secret sauce? I don't know about no secret sauce."

My partner gets an incredulous look on his face and shakes his head. "So," he says, "you want to work at McDonald's, and you don't know about the secret sauce? Wow! Before you apply again you better learn about it."

She went away, but we figure the next twelve times she applies she's going to be driving them bananas about the secret sauce.

YOU'LL ALWAYS BE
RETARDO TO ME
☆

There was a guy named Baccardo, and at the police academy he got the nickname "Retardo." One day a cop who went to the academy with him but whom he hadn't seen for twelve or thirteen years was transferred to the same precinct, and when he recognized Baccardo he yelled out, "Hey, Retardo!"

Another cop comes up to him and says, "Hey, you can't call him that. He's a lieutenant."

"Oh, sorry. Hey, Lieutenant Retardo!"

DERICIOUS

I used to ride with this Chinese cop named Charlie Lai who was really authentic Chinese—born in China, came to America when he was a little boy. He fractured the English language a little, but he was a great cop.

He ate some of the most godawful stuff you could imagine, brains, the eyes of things, dogs, cats, tripe. It makes me shudder to think about it—genuine Chinese cuisine, not Americanized Chinese food, like ribs.

So one day we're in a car on patrol and we park, and he's spooning this stuff—a thin milky liquid with black balls in it—into his mouth. It made me almost hurl, so I say, "How can you eat that crap?"

"What we eat. We eat what we can. You hungry, you eat anything."

So he's almost finished with whatever that mess was, when this guy who's walking his Dalmatian comes near the car, pulled over by his dog. The dog must have smelled the food because he stands up on his hind legs and puts his front paws on the door and starts sniffing like crazy.

I'm a dog lover so I tell the guy, "Beautiful dog."

"Thanks," he says.

"What do you think, Charlie? Beautiful, huh?"

He looks up from his food, looks at the dog, and says, "Rook dericious."

NOT EINSTEIN'S SISTER

☆

I'm telling you," the old-time cop says with heavy disgust in his voice, "the intelligence requirement for new cops has been deteriorating for years. Just a few months ago, me and my partner—she's on the job four months—are involved in a high-speed pursuit. I'm the driver, so she notifies Dispatch about the pursuit, and Dispatch comes back and says they dispatched Aviation.

"She doesn't miss a beat. 'Dispatch!' she says, 'we don't need Aviation! We need a helicopter!'"

WELCOME TO ELMIRA

Back in the '50s a mounted cop from a Bronx precinct was trying to keep warm—it was February, about ten degrees—and he hit on a clever idea. He went over to the freight yards and rode his horse up into one of the freight cars, then closed the door behind him. It was a lot warmer than outside, particularly since he had a bottle with him and he started to nip on it.

He got so comfortable that he fell asleep, and when he wakes up and checks his watch, he realizes he slept for hours. He pulls open the freight-car door and gets another surprise. He sees a sign *Welcome to Elmira*, an upstate town over two hundred miles from the Bronx. I understand he finished off the bottle because he knew he had to call his sergeant and explain why he and his horse were checking out the Elmira freight yards.

Let Me Ease Your Mind, Lad

*A*bout ten o'clock one Sunday morning, this guy named Charlie who operated a bar in midtown was in there sweeping up when he hears a loud knocking on the door. A big Irish sergeant named Mike is there, and he wants to come in. They don't open until twelve o'clock on Sunday, so Charlie points to his watch and shakes his head.

"Open the door," Mike says in his thick Irish brogue.

Charlie goes up to the entrance. "I can't open yet."

"Open the door!"

Reluctantly, Charlie opens the door, and the sergeant goes over to the bar, takes down a stool, and sits on it.

"What do you want?" Charlie asks.

"Bloody Mary. Can't start me day without me Bloody Mary."

Charlie shakes his head. "Sarge, because of the blue laws in New York, you know I can't sell you any alcohol before twelve o'clock. If I do I can lose my license."

"Put your mind at ease, lad," the sergeant says. "I have no intention of paying for it."

MUTILATED
ENGLISH

I made a car stop [pulled a car over] in a bad drug area. The driver is a local drug dealer, and I'm hoping I'll find something. I don't, but I'm still yearning to bust his chops in some way. I had to come up with something. His license is all scratched and barely readable, so I write out a summons for a "mutilated license." I hand him the ticket, and he looks at it and says, "What did you give me a ticket for?"

"For your license. It's mutilated."

"Yo, man. That's [bleep]. My license doesn't mutilate for another six months!"

AND I'LL BE ON MY WAY

During the Dinkins Administration in the '90s, it was the wild west in New York City, with over 2,100 homicides a year. So they come up with a brilliant idea, the Gun Buyback plan. The administration announces it's going to buy guns, "no questions asked," even if the weapon had no serial numbers or was used for a murder. The goal was just to get the guns off the street.

Me and my partner are on a foot post, and a passerby points to a guy walking down the block and says: "He's got a gun!"

The guy who is supposed to have the gun is heading down a one-way street, so we get on the radio and tell Central to get a car to block the other end. When the guy sees the cops coming down the one-way street, he turns and runs—almost right into our arms. "Where you going?" I asked him.

"I'm goin' to the precinct for the buyback program. Handing in my gun."

"Then why you runnin' from us?"

"Got to get there quick! But now that you here, why don't you give me the money, and I'll be on my way!"

NOW THAT'S DANGEROUS!

☆

This old-time cops says, "Today I hear cops complain about having to make five or six runs a night. In the late '80s, when I was on the job, we made fourteen, fifteen runs a night, and half of those were gun runs. It was either shots fired, man with a gun, or when we'd get there we'd see bullet holes, blood, or a body. Listen, let me put it this way: When I was on the job it was so dangerous the Statue of Liberty had both hands up!"

FRAMED

I was on a foot post one beautiful summer night, and naturally there were wall-to-wall people on the street, including lots of tourists. There was this homeless guy who was part of the scene, and he went by the name "Brokejaw" because of his permanently twisted jaw. He was fifty, maybe sixty. He wasn't pretty—he had that jaw and maybe two teeth—but he was harmless. He would walk around with a pushcart filled with his stuff and earn money panhandling. And he had a sense of humor. He made people laugh by pulling his bottom lip over his top one so far it would cover half his nose.

Anyway, a call comes over the radio about an attempted child abduction. I race to the location and find a hysterical woman with a baby in a carriage. She said a guy just tried to take her baby, and she gives me the description. I know right away it is probably Brokejaw. Another unit shows up and takes the woman in a patrol car to canvass the area. I walk to a small park, and I find him. I say, "Hey, Brokejaw.

THE FUNNIEST COP STORIES EVER

This woman says you tried to steal her baby. What happened?"

"Well," he says, "I was lookin' for money in the pay phone, but this lady was standing there with her back to me. I just was gonna move her baby carriage out of the way so I can get to the coin return. She turned around, saw my hand on the carriage, and started screaming, 'Ahhhhh!' So I got scared and yelled, 'Ahhhhhh!' Then she yelled, 'Help me! He's trying to take my baby.' So I got scared, screamed again, grabbed my cart, and ran."

I am laughing at this story because I can see it unfolding as he's telling it. She pulls up in the patrol car and starts yelling, "That's him, that's the guy who tried to take my baby."

We explain to her what happened, that the guy is harmless. She admits she's from the country, and she may have overreacted being this is her first time in the city. The sector car offered to give her a ride back to her hotel, and I walk over to Brokejaw to tell him everything is okay. With that he pulls an old wooden picture frame out of his cart, puts it around his neck, and starts yelling, "I didn't do it! I was framed!"

Learning from an Expert

The thing about being a rookie is that you want everyone to think you have ten years on the job. It's either an ego thing, or you want the perps to think you are a seasoned veteran so they take you more seriously. Or maybe you just want the public to think you know what you're doing even when you are clueless.

Back in the early '90s, when I was a rookie, I collared some dude for whatever and took him back to the station house to print him. At the time I sucked at fingerprinting and would end up getting ink all over me, but I had to do it because it was my collar.

I take the perp out of his cell and start printing him—unsuccessfully. I am doing the fourth or fifth print card when the sergeant yells and asks me when I'm going to be finished. This doesn't help, but suddenly the perp says, "Geez, at this rate I'll be here all night. Let me [bleeping] do it myself."

Then he proceeds to print himself quickly and efficiently—the best prints I've ever seen. He said he does it all the time as a courtesy for rookies. Nice when you can get an expert to help you.

A REAL GOURMET

Some guys you arrest are so experienced with how the prisons in New York work that they could write a [bleeping] guidebook. I got a good example of this about ten years ago when I got a call of a "holding one" in Caldor's, which basically means they're holding a shoplifter, small-time petty larceny stuff. When I get to the store, the manager says this perp has been hitting them pretty often, so instead of taking the stuff back and releasing him, they want to press charges.

I take the guy to the station house, but he is being difficult. He has no ID, and he is not talking. He can't get a desk appearance ticket without proper ID, so we have to send him through the system, starting with taking his prints. The guy keeps moving his hands and screwing up his prints. So I am getting pretty pissed at this B.S. collar, and I yell, "The longer you keep on delaying me printing you, the longer you're going to stay down at central booking!"

He gives me a big toothy smile, shakes his head, and says, "I don't care. They got real good sandwiches down there!"

WITH FRIENDS LIKE THIS, WHO NEEDS ENEMIES?

Go figure this one out. One day me and my partner respond to a burglary in progress. When we arrive at the location a neighbor explains that the home-owners are away. They observed a guy entering through the back door, and he hasn't come out. We enter the house with guns drawn and clear room to room downstairs. Then go upstairs and check the rooms. In one of them, we find the guy. He is lying under the covers in bed. My partner strips off the blanket while I keep him covered. He is fully clothed, boots and all. "Hey," I ask, "what's the deal?"

"Hey, what you all doin' in my house?"

"This ain't your house."

"Well," he says, "it's my best friend's house, I'm watchin' it for him."

We nod and start to cuff him, and then I ask him about the bags near the bed. "And what about all the electronic equipment in the garbage bags?"

"Oh," he says, "that's my boy's stuff. I'm gonna take it to the repair shop tomorrow."

"But tomorrow is Sunday," I say.

"Well, my other friend gots a shop. He opens for me only on Sunday!"

We take him to the precinct and put him in the Graybar Hotel. Once in, he starts pleading his case to two other guests there. They are sympathizing with him, and as I get ready to print him, I hear him say in a high plaintive voice, "They locked me up because I was in my cousin's house!"

I can't help but say, "But you told me that it was your best friend's house."

He looks at me with a mystified look on his face, "Yo, five-0. My cousin is my best friend!"

I Sign Twice!

Back in the '70s, I was on the job in the 109 near Shea Stadium in Queens, where the New York Jets used to play. Some of the players rented apartments near the stadium and threw wild parties. Every once in a while it would get a little loud and the neighbors would call us. We would get there and see Joe Namath being the life of the party with two girls on each arm. Anyway, we get a call one night to tell them to quiet down a bit, and after we answered the call—Namath was there as usual—stopped at this twenty-four-hour diner we frequented. It was managed by a nice Greek immigrant named Nick who spoke broken English and didn't know much about America, but he was very eager to learn.

We start talking about how we just saw Joe Namath. He says in his thick Greek accent, "Who is this Namath? What does he do?"

"Are you kidding, Nick?" I say. "He is the quarterback for the New York Jets. His signing bonus alone is more than you make in ten years."

"What is this signing bonus?"

"Well, when you sign a contract you get a bonus."

"You mean just for signing your name they pay you in this country?"

"Yes. They paid him over four hundred thousand dollars."

"Four hundred thousand dollars just for signing his name?" His face brightened. "Wow," he says, "I sign twice!"

OUTDOOR LOONY BIN

I used to work in the Green Street area back in the '80s. Now it is all redone and full of yuppies, but back then it was an outdoor loony bin. Part of the scene was a homeless woman, around seventy, whose name was Dahlia. She was harmless, though personal hygiene was not her strong suit, and she had lots of road on her face. We would see her for a week, then not see her for a few days—and eventually she would show up wearing a hospital bracelet, a sign that she had been a guest at the psycho ward.

We treated her well. We would give her change once in a while or get one of the bodegas to give her some coffee. One night around Christmas she comes up to me as I am getting into my patrol car.

"Merry Christmas, Offica. Gimme a dollar so I can eat."

"No, I will take you inside and get you a slice of pizza."

"Pizza? I don't eat pizza. I eat rice and beans."

So I take out a buck, and she says, "Gimme two dollars, it's Christmas."

"Two dollars! Okay, but you are taking advantage of me."

She smirks, takes the two dollars, drops her head, and as she walks away turns back and says, "Okay, now find me a boyfriend."

HE'LL SEE ME THEN

I was in the community policing unit back in the early '90s. It's a unit that basically addresses all the conditions that people complain about—gangs, double-parked cars, drugs, prostitution, whatever. The idea was to schmooze with the public and fix the condition so everyone was happy. We go into the stores, schools, houses of worship, and get to know everyone.

The only fly in the ointment was this one maniac sergeant who looked and acted like Barney Fife and who nobody could stand him. He was always looking to hang somebody for something stupid. So one time he has this cop, Cory Bayhill, in his crosshairs. Cory was a good cop with about eighteen years in and one of the best schmoozers on the job. We are doing paperwork just before we go out one day, and this sergeant comes into the room to confront and possibly embarrass Cory. "Hey, Bayhill, what are you doing in the station house?"

Bayhill doesn't even look up and says, "I'm finishing updating my conditions log."

"Well, you always have an excuse for being in here. You should be out on your beat."

Bayhill didn't answer.

"Just so happens I checked on one of the stores on your beat—the piano store. Guy says he hasn't seen you in months."

Bayhill finally looks up. "Well," he says, "when I need a piano he'll see me."

Dumbbells

*O*ne night we respond to a burglary in progress. We get to the scene and start looking in windows and listening for any further screaming—which prompted the complaint—to verify it. The light is dim, but my partner sees there is a guy on the floor kneeling near what appears to be someone tied upside down on a weight bench. We head for the back door, kick it down, and run to the room where the guy is. Then we bum rush him and cuff him. I turn on the lights, and it's a female tied upside down. Her clothes are off, she's gagged, and she has a look of terror in her eyes. I think, what kind of animal would do this? Then I remove the gag, and the woman yells, "We were role playing, please untie me and let my boyfriend go!"

WHO DRESSES YOU?

☆

I was in the Narcotics Enforcement Unit in South Central, and one night during a street-level narcotics operation, we move onto a corner and put like half a dozen people against the wall. I start patting this young kid down, and in his back pants pocket I find a baggie of crack. He immediately says, "It ain't my crack."

I'm cuffing him and say, "Oh yeah, well what's it doing in your pocket?"

"It ain't my pants!"

EYE SEE

We get a call about a fight in the street at East 29th and Lemon. We pull up, and a large crowd is watching a shoplifter and another person duke it out. We know it's a shoplifter because in the middle of summer, he is wearing a shoplifter's overcoat with numerous hidden pockets. The stolen stuff is spilling out as he fights. His opponent is a little Italian guy. We find out later he's the manager of a Safeway and he caught this jerk stealing. They battled inside the store, then spilled out onto the avenue.

Before we can stop the fight, the manager hauls off and hits the thief square in the jaw with a roundhouse right. The shoplifter's glass eye pops out onto the street. He stops fighting and is panicking, trying to find his glass eye. People are screaming, and you could see right into his head. He finally finds his eye, but could not pop it back in. So he says to the store manager, "I'm coming back with a gun, and I'm going to kill you!"

So my partner says, "Well, you better keep an eye out for us, too!"

INVESTING 101

City cops are usually working without a contract, which is why most have second jobs and are always struggling financially. It is a political game. The city offers a low increase so they can hold onto money for two years while the contract gets dragged into arbitration and finally settled. Then the cops get a retroactive paycheck for the raise, which could be as much as a few grand before taxes. The city offers a 457 deferred compensation plan, which is like a 401k plan. The smart thing to do is to put the retro check into deferred comp to avoid high taxes. So one day we were all talking about it when fellow cop and known gambler John Davit walks in. John would bet on raindrops racing down a window. One cop says, "Yeah, I put all I can into the 457 plan."

Another cop says, "Me too, that's the best way to go. What about you, John?"

"Well, yeah, I kind of put it in my own 457 plan. I put it down on the four and the five horse in the seventh at Belmont."

You Have to Install It Correctly

*B*eing a detective in a Chicago precinct is like Forrest Gump's line about a box of chocolates: "You never know what you're going to get." One time, a sweet-looking lady in her early sixties walks into the squad room. She looks very concerned, so I greet her with a smile and ask what I can do for her. She says, "I want to make a complaint about my landlord."

"What did he do?"

She looks around like she has a secret and tells me, "Well, he is breaking into my apartment."

I am thinking this is legit and can be serious, so I should find out more. "Well. What is he doing, is he stealing things?"

"No, nothing is missing."

"Is he watching you?"

"No."

She leans closer and tells me in a hushed voice, "When I leave my apartment, he comes in and rearranges all my Precious Moments figurines."

Now I am trying not to laugh because I can see she is a lonely older lady. I say, "Change the locks."

"I did. He comes through the walls."

"You mean he broke through a hole in the walls?"

"No! He can pass through walls."

"Oh, well, just put tin foil on your walls."

She looks at me like I am crazy. "Tin foil?"

"Yeah, we get this problem all the time. Tin foil is metal. They can't pass through metal. So just put it on the wall he is coming through like wallpaper."

She kisses my hand and says thank you so much. Two weeks later I get a call from her again, and she says it didn't work. He is still passing through her walls. I ask, "Did you put the shiny side facing the wall?"

"No. Does it matter?"

"Of course it matters. The shiny side is what repels."

"Okay, I'll switch it right now."

I guess it kept the landlord out, because I never heard from her again.

THE LEGAL DEFINITION

The academy can be a lot of fun, but they do throw a lot of stuff at you, and memorizing all of it can be a little tough at times. Halfway through the training our law instructor, who was impeccable about defining things, got transferred to another detail. She was replaced by another instructor named Littles, who was a giant. He stood about six-foot-seven or six-eight and he played on the police basketball team. He was also a great guy and a seasoned cop, born and raised in the city—he knew the ways of the street. He came to the academy to teach but also to study for the sergeant's exam.

On the first day, he walks into the class, and everyone is silent looking at him.

"Okay, where did you guys leave off?"

One recruit raises his hand and says, "Robbery."

"Robbery, okay, who can give the definition of robbery?"

One recruit says, "When there is a threat of violence?"

A little girl from the suburbs looks it up in the legal dictionary, raises her hand, and says, "Robbery is the direct taking of property (including money) from a person (victim) through force, threat, or intimidation. Robbery is a felony (crime punishable by a term in state or federal prison). Armed robbery involves—"

He stops her right there. "Take out your books and write this down."

Everyone goes for their books, and Littles says, "Definition of robbery. Somebody comes over to you, punches you in the face, and takes your [bleep]! Dat's robbery! Next chapter."

SECRET AGENT MAN

There was this one cop, a friend of mine named Mark Brenner. He just got transferred to our precinct, and when you get transferred you usually get the lousy details until you get to know the guys and the area. One day he gets the 59th Street Bridge post. They give him a car and tell him to just wait at the base of the bridge to be on terrorist alert type stuff. So he is sitting there for about two or three hours and a call comes over, "108 bridge car on the air."

"On the air, go ahead."

"There is a suspicious male on the bridge. Check and advise."

"Ten-four."

Mark is about six-seven and a good cop. He has a very quick sense of humor and is always using it. He responds, and he sees a guy at the edge of the bridge getting ready to jump. Mark says, "Hey pal, what's going on?"

The guy is a complete EDP. He's crazed, and he starts screaming, "Get back, there are so many spies here!"

"What spies?"

"Spies! All over! I need to get to the right people in government to warn them. I can't trust anyone. They are after me and my information."

Just then another unit pulls up, and the guy turns his attention to them and continues the same rant. With that, Brenner jumps him. They are wrestling on the bridge, and the guy is screaming: "Leave me alone, I need to warn the government!"

The guy has EDP strength. (It is amazing how strong these people are when they have all that adrenaline rushing through them.) Brenner is about to lose him, but he whispers in the guy's ear, "I know you are right. They are all around us."

The guy lightens up a bit so Brenner continues, "I'm with the government, Donald Rumsfeld sent me. He needs to talk to you right away."

The guy stops resisting and straightens up with amazing calmness and says, "Really?"

"Yeah, but you can't tell anyone, or they won't let me take you to him. You have to go peacefully."

The guy looks at the other two officers and says, "Okay, I'll go, but I am only going with Officer Brenner." Then he looks at Brenner and salutes before he lets him put the cuffs on.

I Don't Want to Know

*T*his old timer Bob Fahey told me about a call he went on back in the mid '60s. Boy, does it show how different things were. He was doing a four-to-twelve when he and his partner get a call for a domestic dispute. He gets there, and the husband is tanked and starting all kinds of trouble but nothing violent. Fahey and his partner tell the guy to go sleep it off somewhere and don't come back tonight. They leave, and about two hours later, they get another call. They go back and see that the husband had returned and is still smashed. They tell the guy again to go sleep it off.

"If we have to come back here," one of them says, "we will handle it ourselves."

They leave again and sure enough, about forty-five minutes later they get a third call. They show up, and they say that's it. They put the guy in cuffs, but he's so wasted they're afraid to put him in the car because he might puke all over everything. So they escort him to the car, and put him in the trunk and take off, intending to drop him someplace safe. They are on the expressway, but they are slowed down because of a traffic jam. There is a car broken down in the middle lane, and when they get there, they are shocked: It's the chief's car.

This chief is a real old timer. Irish guy with white hair who came on in the '40s. He has a flat tire and flags down Fahey.

"Officer, I was coming back from a wedding with my wife, and we got a flat tire. I need a jack—I don't have one in my car."

"I'd rather not open the trunk, sir."

"What? Did you hear what I said? Open your trunk!"

"Sir, I am afraid I can't do that."

The chief is getting pretty pissed. "Officer, I am not asking you, I am telling you. Give me the keys, and I'll do it myself!"

The chief grabs the keys and opens the trunk. He stares at the contents for a few seconds, closes the trunk, and yells for his wife to come over. His wife goes to the trunk, and the chief opens it and shows her what's in it. "See, this is why I drink!"

He shuts the trunk, gives the keys back, and Fahey starts to tell him what's going on.

"I don't want to know," the chief says. "Just get out of here and make sure you send me a car with a jack in it!"

COLLAR OF THE CENTURY

There was one cop named Malone who was always kissing ass to try to get into the detective squad. He was always up there in the squad room trying to get his gold shield. He usually exaggerated what he did too. If he collared a jaywalker, he would make it sound like he was lucky to escape with his life. So one day this guy comes into the station house and says to Malone, "You know all those push-in robberies that are in the papers? I did them!"

"Really?"

"Yes."

Excited, Malone brings him upstairs to the detectives' room and tells them that he's got the guy who did the robberies in the neighborhood. The detectives know this guy. He's lonely and a little nutty, and he confesses to a crime every week for the attention. No one lets on about this to Malone, but one of them comes over to the "perp" and says, "You did these robberies, huh?"

"Yeah."

"And did you also have something to do with the homicides in the pizza joint last week? And the three rapes over by the park?"

"Yes."

Now Malone starts to think he's collared the criminal of the century, but the next line tells him everyone is playing a joke on him.

"And how about Son of Sam? You were his accomplice, right?"

"Absolutely!"

Malone gets a look on his face like he's a total fool. Everyone laughs and he storms out of the room. The last thing he heard was one of the cops saying, "And you killed Kennedy, didn't you?"

"Yes, I sure did." And now even Malone was laughing.

MÉNAGE À TROIS

Me and my partner were in the Seven-Three, and we get flagged down by a crowd of people around a bus. A woman tells us there's a guy under the bus. I look in under the bus and spot a big guy who seems okay. "What's going on?" I ask.

"Romeo's trying to kill me."

"Okay, why don't you come out from under the bus, and we'll talk about it."

He rolls out and turns violent. Me and my partner start fighting with the guy. My partner lands a good shot to his nose, and it starts to bleed. He stops fighting instantly and starts wailing, "Oh no! Oh no. Look what you did to this pretty face!"

He starts fighting again, and with some other cops who've arrived we succeed in subduing him. Finally, two of us cuff him, and he announces in a kind of surprised, high, sexy voice, "Oh my goodness! A ménage à trois!"

America's Most Wanted

*N*ew York City is so congested that the police department tries to avoid high-speed chases. So as not to alert the public you're going after someone, you tell Central that you're "observing someone," not that you are going seventy miles an hour to do it.

Once two cops were involved in a chase and got in an accident. The sergeant, who needed the info for his report, asks them, "What happened?"

"We swerved to avoid a dog, and at the last second we hit a parked car."

"Okay, I'll write it up."

Two days later, there is another accident involving two completely different cops, and again the sergeant asked, "So what happened?"

"Same thing as the other day," one cop says, "a dog came out of nowhere and we swerved to miss him and hit a parked car."

The sergeant is getting pissed. That night there's yet another accident, and at roll call he goes into a mini tirade, saying that they lost three cars in two days and telling everyone you got to be careful. Then he starts going into the conditions report for the precinct telling us what to be on alert for: robbers in the area, rapists, you name it. Then a Chinese cop we nicknamed "G," one of the funniest guys I ever met, says in his thick accent, "Hey, Sarge, you rooking for rapists, robbers, murderer, terrorist. Never mind them. You should be rooking for the dog. He the most dangerous person in the city!"

POLICE LINE – DO NOT CROSS   POLICE LINE – DO N

GOOD & WACKY

There was this one cop I knew who was really burnt out. He had been in a couple of shootouts, served in the worst area of the city. He had seen a lot—maybe too much—and he just wanted off the job. Like that character in *M*A*S*H* who dressed like a woman, he did various wacky things like taking cars out with very little gas in them and running them around until they ran out of gas. Then he'd walk back to the precinct, and the sergeant or somebody would say to him, "Where's your car?"

"Ran out of gas."

The police department doesn't know if he's faking or not, they have to take everything seriously. So they take the cars away from him and put him on a foot post. The first day, he goes to a house where a woman has complained about vandalism to her mailbox, and he starts to take the report. While he's doing that, he asks the lady, "Can I use your bathroom?"

"Sure," she says. "No problem."

So he goes into the bathroom, and she waits a few

minutes and then she hears the shower going. A few minutes later he comes out of the bathroom wet, totally nude except for a towel around his waist with his gun belt holding it up, and his hat on.

Freaking out, she calls the precinct, gets the sergeant, and tells him that the officer took a shower in her house. The sergeant rushes over and says to the cop, "What are you doing?"

The cop looks back at the sergeant like he's the one with a couple of screws loose and says, "She said I could use the bathroom."

So he gets dressed, and the sergeant takes him back to the station house. He is too whacked to put on the street, so he's parked at a desk in the complaint room for a month. Then it's time for him to qualify with his weapon, something all cops have to do.

He goes to the range, aims the revolver, and it doesn't fire, so the instructor says, "Draw and present."

The guy opens the chamber and hands the gun to the instructor, who sees there is candy where the bullets should be. Pink in one chamber, white in the next, then pink, then white.

The instructor says, "You know you got Good & Plentys in here?"

"Ah, [Bleep]! The kids were playing with my gun again!"

That was his ticket out.

WHY SHE ISN'T MARRIED

I was once in plainclothes, and I stopped to look in a store window. There was a homeless black guy about sixty going through a trash basket on the corner, and standing near him was a heavyset middle-aged woman with heavy makeup, all dressed up and very snobbish looking. She is on a cell phone, and the homeless guy pauses in his excavation and says, "Excuse me, Miss, could you spare some change?"

She keeps talking, acting like this homeless guy doesn't exist. He repeats the question when she hangs up, and instead of answering it, she starts on a tirade about capitalism. "You wouldn't have to panhandle if you got a job, etc., etc."

When she's finished, the homeless guy eyes her up and down and says, "Now I know you're not married."

"Why? Because I'm not wearing a ring?"

"No. Because you're ugly."

Close Call

*W*e get a call from a woman who says there's a dispute at a certain address and that the super is threatening a tenant with a gun. She doesn't give us a callback number so we can't verify the call, but we have to treat every complaint seriously. We call for backup, go to the super's basement apartment, and knock on the door.

"Who is it?" a man answers.

"Police! Open up!"

"Okay. One minute."

Then we hear a mechanical *ka-chuk* that sounds exactly like a shell being racked into a shotgun. As he goes to open the door, we kick it down and start roughing him up and cuffing him. "Where's the [bleeping] gun? Where's the gun?"

"Wait a minute. What gun? I have no gun!"

We look around his little apartment. He's got pictures of American scenes, American heroes, the flag. We can't find a gun. "We heard a gun. Sorry."

He is a little shaken, but he says, "No problem. No problem."

He walks us to the door, and as we start to leave, he pulls the string controlling the light. We hear a *ka-chuk*—which sounds just like a shotgun being racked.

A
SERIOUS MALADY
☆

A motor vehicle fatality occurred, and me and my partner Frank responded. It's a bad scene, very bad. Turns out that one of the two drivers, a female, has been decapitated. She is visible, and I quickly cover her up while Frank went over and pushed the crowd back. A few minutes later, he comes walking toward me, his back to the crowd, and he's got a big grin on his face. Frank is normally a pretty serious kind of guy, so I wonder what's up. He says, "When I was pushing the crowd back this young girl comes up to this young guy who's apparently her boyfriend and says, "What's going on, Tony?"

"A woman in the car was decaffeinated."

I had to turn away so the crowd couldn't see me busting a gut.

"[BLEEP] YOU! [BLEEP] YOU!"

In his book *Soul of a Cop*, hero cop Paul Ragonese tells the story of a woman who came into the Twenty-Third precinct and told the cops that her boyfriend was holding their eight-year-old boy hostage in his apartment. Uniformed cops immediately went to the apartment and demanded that the guy open up.

The response, in a Spanish accent, was "[Bleep] you!" The detectives tried to convince the guy to open the door, and all they got was the same "[Bleep] you! [Bleep] you!" So they called ESU [Emergency Service Unit].

The situation played out for three hours, during which time crowds had gathered, a helicopter hovered overhead, and the media was coming out of the woodwork.

After three hours, all the cops had gotten when they asked the guy to come out was "[Bleep] you!"

Finally, they decided to take down the door and try to pull the kid out. Ragonese and his partner used sledgehammers on the door, and then other cops armed with shotguns rushed in yelling, "Freeze, police!" They were met with another "[Bleep] you" coming from behind a closed bedroom door.

Fed up, the cops yelled for the guy to come out—and again were told "[Bleep] you."

They took the other door down and discovered that the guy was gone. Staring at them was an innocent little dark brown, yellow-billed Mynah bird that again told them "[Bleep] you! [Bleep] you!" in a Spanish accent. Turns out the boyfriend had left the apartment hours earlier and the boy was home. Soon after, one of the cops told the complainant that the best thing she could do was to get rid of the bird.

THREE STARRING LING GI

I had a Chinese partner named Ling Gi who was a great guy and a very good cop. He had been a transit cop, and he rode the A line, which was the toughest in the city. I was involved in more funny incidents with "G," as we called him, than you could imagine. Here are three of the many stories that kept me in stitches.

One day we're driving along on Northern Boulevard, and I see an old lady waving us down. I pull over and G starts yelling at me in this thick Chinese accent.

"Why you pur over?" he says. "Why you pur over?"

"She's waving us down."

"She just going to ask you a stupid question."

"How do you know that? We got to check it out." So I ease up to her and stop.

"How come," she says, "the buses are running late?"

"I don't know, ma'am," I replied.

"Well, can you give me a ride?"

And G says, "This is poreece car. Not taxi."

We drive on two more blocks during which he says nothing. Then he blurts out.

"Pur over. You don't drive no more. I drive."

"Why?"

So we switch seats and he starts driving. "So," I said, "what if somebody waves you down?"

"We wave back!"

"What if you get a CCRB [civilian complaint]?"

"What," he says, "I think she wave at me just to say herro. So I wave back. That's community poreecing. I don't know anything. I'm a stupid Chinaman." And he gives me a little wave.

There are a lot of double parkers in Flushing, which is heavily Asian. One day we stopped so Ling Gi could write a ticket for a double-parked cab driven by a Chinese guy. He says, "Hey, I'm Chinese, you're Chinese. Give me a break."

Ling Gi puts his hand up. "Wo—wo—wo," he says very rapid fire and kind of loud, "I'm Chinese, you Chinese. I'm supposed to give you a break? You my friend? Every Chinaman supposed to know every other Chinaman? Give every other

Chinaman a break? Why don't you come over and sreep with my wife? Would that be okay? Good enough? Who you? I don't know you! And now you get two tickets."

Me and G were in plainclothes detail giving peddlers summonses. Stores complain about them because they don't pay taxes or rent and it's illegal —dishonest competition.

We stopped for lunch in a Chinese restaurant, and there was an old couple at one of the tables. At one point Ling Gi says, "I got to wash my hands," and starts for the bathroom. His route takes him right by the old couple and the woman says, "Waiter, can you get us some water?"

G stops, smiles, and says, "Oh. You think I'm waiter? All Chinese people the same, right? All waiters! Ching chong, ching chong! How about you? You old, you ready to play shuferboard. Everybody do the same thing? We got shuferboard in back room. C'mon, ret's go?"

He waits for an answer, which he doesn't get, then heads away toward the bathroom—or to play shuffleboard alone.

TOP FIVE
COP PRANKS

1. Loosening the nut on a urinal water pipe at the staion house. This results in the officer standing at the urinal getting a mini bath with his clothes on.

2. Smearing black ink on the holes in the black phone receiver used by the desk officer, so when he answers the phone, ink transfers to his ear, and he spends a lot of time wondering why people are looking at his ear.

3. Gluing the zipper shut on the riot helmet bag so it can't be opened and either has to be ripped open or the glue removed out from between the zipper teeth, a truly labor-intensive job.

4. Placing mice in the patrol car. Particularly effective with female officers.

5. Placing baby powder in the patrol car A/C vents. When the driver starts the car with the A/C on full blast, he or she turns white.

No Parking in Alley

*W*e had one guy, let's call him Knoll, who would give his mother a summons for a traffic infraction. I mean he would even ticket another cop, and he did. He was probably psychotic or something—he issued over a hundred summonses a month. When other cops approached him and told him to knock it off, he didn't listen, so we decided it was time to do the nasty on him.

One night he comes in and goes to his locker as usual, and there is a problem. It's not there. The locker is six feet high and two feet wide, and it can't walk away on its own. "Where's my locker?" Knoll announces to a crowd. A lot of guys had showed up just to see his reaction. No one laughed or responded except Brown, a very funny guy, says, "Maybe it was stolen. You have valuables in it? Maybe a couple of cases of summonses?" This gets a big laugh.

"[Bleep] you," Knoll says.

"What are you getting out of joint for?" Brown says. "Just report it missing to the detective squad." Another laugh.

Knoll stomps out of the locker room, goes into the captain's office, and starts complaining. The captain goes through the motions but does nothing. He knows Knoll is a psycho, and doesn't want a lot of other cops pissed at him. So Knoll himself searches all over the precinct for the locker, and he finally finds it. It is two stories down in the alley, all bent and broken; it had been thrown out the window. To add insult to injury, somebody had taped three summonses to it and had written under the infraction part, "No parking in alley."

SUBWAY PEEP SHOW

Of course, you meet all kinds of weirdos on the job, including perverts galore.

One who always stood out in my mind was a guy I spotted on the Lexington Avenue subway station at Forty-Second Street. I was on plainclothes duty. We always scope people out, but when I first saw this guy standing on the platform, he didn't seem anything special to me. Quite the contrary. He was a well-dressed middle-aged man with a tie and shirt and wearing a nice fedora and camel hair overcoat. He was standing a couple of feet from the edge of the platform, facing the tracks.

A train came into the station as I went about my business, but when it left I was surprised to see the guy still there. So I made myself as invisible as I could and watched the new train come in. When it pulled to a stop, I saw this guy's head swiveling back and forth like he was checking out who was getting on and off the train. The doors finally closed and the train left the station. Without him. I thought maybe we had an EDP.

Another train comes into the station, and he does this head swiveling thing again. Then I see him take a few steps so he's standing next to one of the windows. I can also see a pretty woman is sitting there.

The doors closed, and a millisecond before the train starts to pull out, I see him open his camel hair coat, and spread it apart. The woman in the window looks his way and freaks out. As the train passes me I see her looking back, her arms waving, screaming.

The train goes into the tunnel, and by then he has closed and rebuttoned the coat. But he stays on the platform. I sidle up to him, flash my tin, and say, "Hey, pal, what you got in that coat?"

"Nothing."

"Let me see."

He opens the coat, and the answer was right. Nothing. His pants, overlapped by the bottom of the coat, only went to mid thigh and were attached to the bottom of his shirt with suspenders. From the waist to the pants he was totally naked. Cops who heard about it called it "The Subway Peep Show."

AND OUT IT COMES

We had this desk sergeant—let's call him Lou—who was a good guy, and sometimes he'd pull pranks on us. Some other guys devised a prank to really nail him. We knew a homeless guy with one good arm and one false arm that looked pretty real unless you were up close. We knew the arm could be detached, so we bribed the guy to become part of the prank.

One night me and my partner bring this homeless guy into the station like he's a regular collar. I'm on one side of him and my partner's on the other. We approach the desk and just before we get there, as planned, the homeless guy makes a dash for it and I grab his arm and pull on it and out it comes—it looks like it came out of the socket. I keep the arm sort of out of sight so Lou can't be sure it's false, and the homeless guy hits the ground and starts yelling.

"Give me my [bleeping] arm back. Give me my [bleeping] arm back! You ripped my [bleeping] arm out of the socket!"

I look at Lou like I don't know what to do. He's standing up, his face is white as a sheet. He doesn't know what to do either. I say, "Should I call a doctor?"

"What?" Lou says. Then he gets it, and he laughs as hard as anyone else.

Double Jeopardy

One New Year's Eve in the mid '90s, I was doing a four-to-twelve and was also driving the patrol supervisor (a sergeant) around. It was pretty quiet for a New Year's Eve until around eleven P.M., when we get notified of a dispute on Briggs Street. A sector car was already there, but they wanted the patrol sergeant at the scene because there was a possible mental case involved, and a superior officer is required.

We arrive at the scene. It is an upscale apartment complex, but we know right away where the trouble is. Three people—two middle-aged females and a middle-aged male—are on the grass and they're surrounded by all kinds of things—stereo, dishes, small appliances—that have obviously been tossed by the EDP, who's on a balcony above yelling down at them. One of the women yells up, "Peter, please calm down. It's okay. You're right. We'll do it your way."

The sergeant asks Paul, one of the sector guys, "What set him off?"

Paul says, "Ma'am, you tell him."

"Well, we were going to have a quiet New Year's at home,

have some friends over from his job at the post office, play some board games, and have a few drinks. We decided to play Home Jeopardy."

The guy on the balcony is quiet, but then yells: "I don't have to put the answer in a [bleeping] question! It's my [bleeping] house with my [bleeping] rules!" Then he left the balcony and went back into the apartment.

"Oh," the woman says, "he heard me say 'Jeopardy.'"

We all look at each other and start to laugh. "So?"

The girlfriend continues, "We got to Final Jeopardy, and he didn't put his correct answer in a question so the other couple said he lost. I took their side, so he got angry and started throwing things around in the apartment. Then he started throwing everything over the balcony, and the neighbors called you guys."

A few seconds later the guy is back on the balcony, and he throws more stuff down—pillows, sheets, blankets.

Of course, being NYPD cops, we have to start in with jokes. We all yell up questions with an emphasis on the question part. "Peter, *what's* the matter?"

"*What's* the problem?"

"*Who's* bothering you?"

The sergeant tells us to knock it off, and we do. About a minute later, the ESU shows up, and one of their guys asks, "What's the matter?"

We all just burst out laughing.

ROAD SCHOLAR

I was in the detective squad when I get a call that we had a potential homicide way up on the north end of the precinct by the Whitestone Bridge. I had to notify the CO of the detective squad who was new in the precinct, and he needed directions to the crime scene. I put him on hold a moment and announced, "Anyone know how to give the lieutenant directions from his house in Long Island to the bridge scene?"

Nobody knows. I guess they all lived in the city or something. I am about to tell the lieutenant that nobody knows when I hear a voice from the cage [a cell for prisoners in the station house], "For that last slice of pizza I'll tell ya."

I look up at the guy in the cage. He is neat and clean, and I know he has been collared for GLA [grand larceny auto]. He would steal cars from rich people across the Long Island border and bring them to the city auto shops that would chop them up.

"Go ahead," I said.

So the guy starts rattling off the quickest way to get there and all these alternative routes if there is traffic, and I relay it all to the CO. Then I hang up, and give the guy his slice and ask him, "You're a walking MapQuest. How do you know so much about roads?"

"Hey, I'm good at what I do."

"So how come you got caught?"

He takes a bite of his pizza, munches it slowly, savoring it, and finally says, "I guess you guys are better."

A NEW YORK MOMENT

There a lot of things about New York that make it a great city, but what is really the heart and soul of it is the people. I mean, the different cultures and how even though they are different they take it in stride and get along. I used to love being on a foot post so I could just absorb the whole scene. One of the funniest things I ever witnessed was on Queens Boulevard. I stopped at a pushcart for a bottle of water, and there were two bus drivers there. They were just making small talk about the weather, the women walking around, and stuff like that. One guy was short, balding, heavyset, and white. The other was older, thin, a black guy who resembled Morgan Freeman. The white guy starts to tell his plans for the weekend in his heavy New York accent, which I love.

"Ah geez, I'm goin' away dis weekend, upstate. Gonna do some fishin'."

The black guy asks in his accent, which I

also love, "What kind uh fish you fish foe?"

"I dunno. I don't care. I catch 'em and trow 'em back."

"You what? Dat's crazy! Why don't you eat dem?"

"I don't eat fish. I just find it relaxin' to go on the water and fish."

"Man, you crazy. Go on the water all you want. Row around the whole damn lake if you want. But why you gotta botha the dam fish foe? They ain't botherin' you! How you like it I stick a hook in yo mouth and rip it out then th'ow you back 'cause it 'relaxes me'?"

"Ah, what's da big deal? After a day of it, I sleep like a baby."

"Sleep like a baby? Man I don't understand white folks' expressions. You know what a baby does? It wakes up cryin' every two hours and wets its bed. Is dat what you do? Cry and wet yo bed every two hours? Another thing. I got a friend that goes out east and goes antiquing with his wife. What the hell is dat?"

"If it's nice, dey probably goes to dem expensive estates out in da Hamptons—"

The black guy cuts him off. "Shut up. I know what it is but I don't get it. When a white man has something old it's 'an antique.' When a black man has somethin' old it's 'junk'!"

They agree, finish their dogs, and get on their buses to finish their routes. Man, you gotta love it.

Stopped for Gas

*T*his event occurred in the patrol car when I had a young female partner named Jessy. One fall afternoon, we were driving along Ventura Avenue when I started to feel stomach distress, and there was no mystery about why. For lunch we had stopped at a Korean place, and whenever I eat Korean I get a little gassy. But I was feeling something way beyond what I normally felt. I had a pain in the middle of my stomach like someone was twisting my guts. I knew what the answer was: Pass wind, get the gas out.

Of course, this was a problem because of Jessy. I had one partner who used to fart in the car—not caring about anything—and we almost got into a fistfight over it. I knew I had to stop the car and do it outside if I could. So I said, "I got to stop the car."

"Why?"

"I want to check the engine. I think I heard something."

So I stop the car in a little shopping center where there's no one around, and then go around to the front and open the hood. By this time I am sweating and in real pain. I put hands on the front of the car to brace myself. Jessy can't see me or, more important, hear me because all the windows are closed. Finally I release one of the loudest, longest farts of my life. It sounded like the fog-horn of a freighter.

Before I was finished I hear this high cackling laughter. Two women I hadn't seen are across the street standing in a doorway and they have seen and heard everything. Christ, they were still laughing when I drove away.

THE LEADING
CAUSE OF DEATH
IN FLORIDA

I know one thing about Florida," said a sergeant who retired to Florida.

"What's that?" his ex-partner asked.

"The leading cause of death."

"Which is?"

"The electric chair."

WHAT COLOR FOR YOU?

We got a call to go to Home Depot because a customer was causing a ruckus in the paint department. When we got there, things had more or less calmed down. The customer had threatened one of the employees. It didn't come to blows, but it was close.

The customer didn't handle English too well, and when he arrived, he had marched up to the employee and announced that he wanted to "stain his dick."

The employee kept a straight face and said: "So what color you want? Blue, green, red, natural?" With that he started to cackle, and the customer didn't know why. "Why you laugh?"

"I thought of something funny."

"You laugh at me?"

"Oh no. Never." Then he starts to laugh harder. He basically couldn't control himself.

About then the wife or the girlfriend of the customer comes into the department, and he has a brief conversation in their native language. He finally gets what's going on. So he turned on the employee, yelling at him in his own language, and it starts getting hot. Then another employee calls the manager, and he calls us. But it's a good thing the guy didn't see my face when I heard the story. I was trying to be professional, but I was laughing too hard.

SURVIVAL OF THE FITTEST

One day me and my partner were doing a training gig with a kid who was like two weeks out of the academy—fresh-faced, full of energy and enthusiasm. We figured it was time to introduce him to the world, specifically a guy called Joe and the woman he was always with named Sarah.

They were a homeless couple, totally harmless, but Joe had a nickname. Cops called him "Low Tide" because of his breath. I mean, this guy could hire himself out to remove wallpaper. All he'd have to do would be to stand in the room and breathe for fifteen minutes, and the wallpaper would come off.

We knew where they usually hung out—in this alley on Jacobs Avenue. So we drove over and found them there. We stopped the car and my partner said to the kid, "Eric, see that homeless couple in the alley? They're like alley strays, but they are the eyes and ears in the neighborhood for us. Why don't you go over and introduce yourself."

"Okay!" So he bounds out of the car and walks into the alley straight for Joe and Sarah. Me and my partner are watching him with great interest. Joe looks straight at this kid walking briskly toward him. When Eric gets to within a few feet of Joe, he abruptly turns and starts heading back to us. The expression on his face tells us he's caught a noseful of Low Tide's breath. Me and my partner are hysterical, and when he sees us laughing he gets it, and starts laughing himself. He was a sharp kid.

When he gets into the car he says one word, "Yuck."

"How'd you like your visit?"

"What I can't understand is how anybody can be around that guy all the time."

"Oh, you mean Sarah," my partner says. "Didn't you notice?"

"Notice what?"

"Charles Darwin got in the act. She has no nostrils. Survival of the fittest."

MOMMY, WHERE ARE YOU?

☆

The day Martin Luther King was gunned down was one of the tensest days I ever spent on the job. There were riots or near riots everywhere, and we were called to quell the disturbance near 122nd and Lenox in the heart of Harlem.

It was me, my partner Louie Perlman, and a rookie named Fred Garnet. We had never seen him under pressure, so we had no idea how he was going to react. We're getting close to the scene, and Fred is very quiet, so me and my partner are thinking maybe he's going to go south on us if there's action. So I ask him, "How you doin', Fred?"

"Fine. Would you please do me a favor?"

"Sure."

"Call up my mommy and tell her I need my blankie?"

We burst out laughing, instantly sure he was going to be all right. And he was.

Clothes Don't Make the Man
(or Woman)

*M*e and my partner, Mike Heppernan, were working Anti-Crime in the 109 one night, when a "1010" call for help near the Whitestone Bridge comes in. Anti-Crime is supposed to pick up street crimes by cruising in an unmarked car and blending into the neighborhood, so we're not stylishly dressed. We wear plainclothes, long hair, maybe even a ponytail if we get permission. We are not usually supposed to pick up jobs over the radio, but this night the sector cars were busy, so we took the call. When we show up we hear a woman screaming behind some bushes and we find this twentysomething-year-old girl laying on the ground completely nude. She's yelling from what looks like a bad mescaline trip. "Get off me! Get off me!" Except there's no one on her.

"You all right?" I ask while Mike goes to get a flashlight. Now we're in a desolate area, and when my partner comes out, he sees an old, heavyset woman wearing just a sweatsuit. She looks at him, and suddenly starts blowing a whistle.

Mike yells, "Stop, lady! Stop!"

"Go away," she yells, "get away from her. I'm part of neighborhood watch. If you don't, I'll call the cops."

"Lady," he said, "I am the cops! Stop blowing that whistle in my ear!"

"Where's your uniform?"

"I'm undercover. We don't wear uniforms. Here's my shield."

She stares at him in disbelief and says, "You don't look like a cop with that long hair and torn clothes."

"Yeah, well, you're wearing a sweatsuit, and you don't look like no aerobics instructor!"

OLICE LINE – DO NOT CROSS   POLICE LINE – DO NO

OFFICER YUMMY

One night I was on a foot post in the Sixth in Greenwich Village, and I saw two obviously gay guys coming out of a hallway. One of them was sipping an open can of beer. This is a minor infraction, but the department wants us to crack down on it here, so I approach. "Excuse me, guys," I say, "but drinking in public like that is against the law. You'll either have to throw the can away or put it in a bag and drink it that way."

The guy drinking the beer has on heavy makeup and upswept blonde hair. His eyes are wide, glistening. He looks me up and down and says, "Oh my God, you are delicious!"

At this point, I am a bit taken aback, but I am a New Yorker and I can roll with the punches, so I laugh a little. Before I can tell him again to put the beer away, he grabs his friend by the arm and says, "I want you to meet someone. Isn't the officer delicious?"

His friend starts in too, "Oh, my God yes. He's yummy!"

With that they both start to sing that commercial for

cat food, "Yum yum yum yum yum yum yum yum yum yum yum yum yum yum . . ."

Then they head back into the house to solve the beer problem, and just as they do I see my sergeant getting out of his car to sign my memo book. I am hoping that he did not see the interaction between me and these guys. He signs my book and says, "Where you going now?"

"I'm going to West Fourth, okay?"

I thought I got away with it, but he hands me back my book and says, "Fine, stay safe and see ya later . . . Officer Yummy."

DR. DIRT

There was this cop who had the nickname "Dr. Dirt" because whenever there was a dirty job in the precinct he always got it. I mean, he would be the first at all kinds of homicide scenes—including one where they had to take a body out of a cesspool—as well as motor fatals and just about everything that other people didn't want to do.

He looked like a guy with that nickname, too. He was pretty big with a big belly, very heavy eyebrows, and really intense dark eyes that were always looking at the world in a very cynical way. He had his twenty in, so he could say and do just about anything, and nobody could touch him. If they gave him a hard time, he would just throw in his papers.

He was always telling us how much change he had seen over the years. Not just in the city but in the department itself. How the NYPD was not hiring the same type of tough street cop like it used to. How the job was better back in the old days when he first came on.

So one day in the summer on an eight-to-four day tour, a call about a DOA [dead on arrival] comes in. Turns out this guy who lived alone was mowing his lawn and had a heart attack and died. Well, this being New York in the late '80s, nobody noticed for about two, maybe three weeks. There was a stench in the air, and the lawn was overgrown except where he had died, so the neighbors finally called it in. Now, a dead body in the middle of July exposed to the elements—well, let's just say it was not a pleasant sight or smell. Rats had started in on him, and maggots had already made him their home. Two rookies get the call, did all the paperwork, and waited for the ME. The meat wagon shows up just as these two rooks are being relieved by two other rooks, a guy and a girl, from the four-to-twelve tour. Dr. Dirt is driving the sergeant, and they show up to see what is going on. Six cops were there when the city morgue guys pick up the body and put it in the body bag to take it away. One morgue guy takes the two arms, and the other takes the two legs. They are supposed to count one, two, three and lift and put him in the body bag. As they get to three, the dead guy's arms come off. All four rookies turn away and lose it. One puked, and then it was a chain reaction—they all did.

THE FUNNIEST COP STORIES EVER

Dr. Dirt just calmly lights up his cigar and says to the three guy cops, "What's this job coming to? When I came on the job men were men." Then he turns to the female. "And so were the women!"

Not a Silver Bullet

*I*n his book *My Life in the NYPD: Jimmy the Wags*, Patrick Picciarelli tells this story involving a well-known celebrity.

I was working in the Ninth, the East Village. Back in the '70s, it was referred to as the "Evil." It was very busy this night because it was the middle of a heat wave, and the natives were restless. We were on a midnight-to-eight tour and about four A.M. things started to quiet down. Then right in front of us, we see this Caddy weaving all over the street. We decide to pull him over by Ave B and see what's up. I approach the driver's side, and my partner approaches the passenger side, which is the proper tactics for car stops.

"Hi, Officer," the dark-skinned driver managed to slur.

He looked familiar, but I couldn't put my finger on it. As he handed me his license, he blurted out, "I'm Tonto!"

With that the door flew open, and he vomited all over the street. Sure enough, I looked at his license, and it said he was Jay Silverheels. I couldn't believe it. I grew up watching *The Lone Ranger*. Here I was about to bust his faithful companion. I called to my partner on the other side of the car, "Hey Kenny, we got Tonto here."

He was a very happy drunk and a great guy. Within ten minutes, we had every working car in the command trading "Hows," taking pictures, him signing autographs. He told us some great stories of the show and his life and how he loved Clayton Moore (the Lone Ranger) like a brother. After a few hours and some coffee, he sobered up and "kemo sabed" us to death. We put him back in his car and pointed him to the Brooklyn Bridge, and watching him so we knew he was okay. As he drove off, he stuck his head out of the window and yelled, "Gettum up, Scout!"

Then my partner Kenny says, "Who was that man?"

"I don't know partner, but he left this," and I pointed to the pile of Tonto's vomit in the street.

TOP TEN FUNNY
PRECINCT NICKNAMES

Cops use humor to cope with things. They'll garnish anything with a little humor, and one of the things they love
to do is give the station house a nickname based on its
essential character. What follows is a lineup of ten New
York City precincts, though not in the order of funniness.

1. **112th Precinct**—Fort Bagel. Named for the large Jewish population in the precinct.

2. **75th Precinct**—The Killing Fields. Named for all the
   murders that took place there in the late '80s and early
   '90s. In 1993 there were 126 murders in the 75th.

3. **62nd Precinct**—Fort Goomba. Located in the Benson-
   hurst area of Brooklyn. Named for its wannabe mob-
   sters who are famous for statements like, "Yo, do you
   know who I am?" Followed by, "Do you know who
   I know?"

4. **77th Precinct**—The Alamo. In Brooklyn. Got its name in the '80s because the officers felt as if they were under siege.

5. **41st Precinct**—Fort Apache. Located in the South Bronx, this precinct was in the middle of a burned out, devastated wilderness where hope was a rarity. Some sergeant nicknamed it after the John Wayne cowboys-and-Indians movie *Fort Apache* when he was calling downtown for help because the precinct literally was being assaulted by people living in the area. A film starring Paul Newman called *Fort Apache, the Bronx* made it famous.

6. **114th Precinct**—Fort Souvlaki. Named for the large Greek population in the precinct.

7. **Police Academy**—Fort Pencil.

8. **6th Precinct**—Fort Swish. Located in the heart of Greenwich Village with its large gay population.

9. **66th Precinct**—Fort Surrender. Back in the '80s, a large group of religious Jews were protesting something that had happened in the precinct. The demonstration got out of hand, and the people ended up storming the precinct. A 10-13 [officer needs assistance in a hurry] went out over the station radio. Cops from other

commands had to come in and help take back the station house.

10. **109th Precinct**—Fort Frushing. Located in Flushing, Queens. Got its name for the way the large Asian population constantly mispronounces the name. In the early '90s, there were over seventy ethnic organizations listed within the 109. There was a T-shirt printed up at the time that read, "The last American out of Flushing, grab the flag!"

TIN FOIL, WORKING FOR YOU, INDOORS AND OUT

I was working in the Six-Oh, Brighton Beach, Brooklyn, also known as "Little Odessa" for all the Russian immigrants who relocated there after the fall of the Soviet Union. I had about six months on and was working with Jimmy Sabatino, a real streetwise Brooklyn guy. He was smooth, knew how to handle everything. Sometimes it seemed like nothing fazed this guy. We get a call of a 10-10, which can mean a lot of things. It stands for possible crime, calls for help, whatever. We go to this very old building by the boardwalk, to third-floor apartment 3J. This sixtysomething old Jewish lady answers the door. We ask her what the problem was, and she invites us in and starts to tell us why she called. "Well, I am afraid to leave my apartment because they are out to get me."

Jimmy, in his real thick Brooklynese, goes, "Who's dey?"

"Them."

"Yeah, who's dem?"

The lady points up toward her ceiling. So being a naive rookie, I say, "You mean the people upstairs?"

I'll never forget the look on her face. It was as if I were the crazy one who should be committed. She says, "Noooooo. Not them. The UFO people. They are trying to get to my brain with radio waves."

Without missing a beat, like he has seen this a thousand times, Jimmy says, "Put tin foil on da TV and radio attennas. Den on the windowsill and you should be fine, dear."

"I went to the precinct, and they told me to do the same thing, so I did."

I went over to look at her TV and window, and sure enough there was tin foil. She says, "That isn't the problem. It works in here, but I can't leave my house."

Jimmy walks her to the kitchen and starts up a conversation with all kinds of small talk. He goes in her pantry closet, and she has like twenty boxes of Reynolds Wrap. As he is talking about the weather and how he uses matzoh with his linguini because it is less fattening than bread, he makes her this aluminum-foil hat. The thing looked like a hat Captain Crunch would wear. "Here, dear, put dis on wheneva you go out. Dey can't get radio waves trew it, and you should be fine."

She thanked him up and down, and we leave. The next week, we see her walking outside on the avenue doing her shopping wearing her tin-foil hat and looking like a female Captain Bly. She comes over to the car, "Thank you so much, Jimmy. This hat works great!"

QUOTE FROM A
CLEVELAND HOMICIDE
DETECTIVE'S
OFFICE

A dermatologist knows nothing and does nothing, a surgeon knows something and does something. A medical examiner knows everything—but a day too late.

On the Table, Please

Back in the mid '70s, we made a raid on a gambling game. It was run by wiseguys, and they usually didn't take much crap from anybody. They were always swaggering in one way or another. There was guy on the squad named Carl Benton who was one of the toughest guys I ever met, and he got off one of the best lines I ever heard when we made that raid.

We burst into the cellar where the game was going on, and everybody was told to freeze and put their hands in sight. They all cooperated except one guy, an enforcer without a neck named Tony Bol. It happened in a split second, but he had his hands under the gaming table, and one of the cops yelled for him to get them in sight. He didn't, so Carl runs up to him, cocks his Berreta, holds it against his head, and says softly, "Put your hands or your brains on the table."

His hands came in sight real quick.

THEY ALMOST GOT ME

I was on the Bunco Squad in the late '80s, and I was fortunate to collar some of the Williamson gang, a group of thieves who travel around the country—they're also known as "Travelers"—conning people into buying home improvement work done that is worthless. For example, they come to the house in midday when just a woman is likely to be there and tell her that they will coat the driveway with a can of sealer for sixty dollars. That seems reasonable, so then they apply some kind of junk—it might be used crankcase oil or paint. When they're finished—very quickly—they tell the woman she owes them six hundred dollars. When she protests that they said only sixty dollars they reply, "That's right, sixty dollars a can. We used ten cans."

The woman offers them a check, and they say they only take cash. They accompany her to the bank, and while they're gone, their confederates may rob her house.

I was visiting my older aunt in Queens. While I'm there she answers the door and someone starts giving her a rap about why she needs her roof done. So while this guy is talking, I sneak up behind the door and listen. He was so convincing I was tempted to take him up on it.

Instead, I step out from behind the door with my gun and badge and say, "Where do I sign?"

HOW TO GET TO HORREEKETOPEEKEE

I was doing a foot post day tour in Queens, and a guy approached. He looked like he might be from another country, and when he opened his mouth, I knew he was. He had a heavy accent.

"Help me go somewhere," he says.

"What do you mean?"

"Go somewhere."

Then I get it. He wants directions to go somewhere. "Where do you want to go?"

"Two-three-oh-four Horreeketopeekee."

I repeat what he said, and he nods. "I'm sorry," I said, "I don't know where that is."

"Oh."

Then something dawns on me. "You have the name written out?"

He takes a piece of paper from his breast pocket and hands it to me. I look at it and burst out laughing. On it is written "2304 Jericho Turnpike."

POLICE LINE - DO N... OLICE LINE - DO N

For Crowd Control

*O*ne mounted cop had a clever way of getting off the street with his horse. He and the horse would get on one of those street freight elevators, and it would lower them to the cellar. He'd tether the horse to something downstairs and go on his merry way for a few hours. When he returned, it was a simple matter for him and the horse to be lifted to the street, and he's on his way back to the barn. But one time when he returned it wasn't so simple because the horse had died. There was no way he could move a thousand-pound animal onto the elevator.

Me and the guys sat around making up reasons he could give his sergeant about why he had gone down there. The best I heard was "crowd control." His sergeant would say, "There are no people down in the cellar."

"No," he would answer. "But hundreds of rats."

DUELING REMOTES

One day we were driving on West Covina when we get a call that there's a disturbance a few blocks away, a woman is calling for the second time about neighbors yelling and fighting.

We go to the apartment, and we can hear loud arguing in the hallway. We knock on the door and this old Irish guy opens up. We tell him that we got a complaint about noise. "Yeah," he says, "it's all Mamie's fault."

"Who's Mamie?"

"The bitch I married."

And from the room we hear, "I heard that, you old bastard!"

"Sure, lads, come on in."

We go inside and meet the wife and ask them what's going on. They start jawing at each other about how she hates how he uses his remote, pressing the change button a "mile a minute." So she sometimes uses her remote to turn the TV off, which makes him turn it back on, and then they just duel—the TV going on and off.

139

So far, each of them have mysteriously lost four or five remotes.

We know they're eccentric, but we have to come up with a solution. So I stop their arguing and say, "Look, we are too busy to come here again. Sir, you watch TV in one room, and lady, you watch it in here."

They are silent, but they look kind of sad.

"What's wrong?"

"But we'll miss each other."

Proof That Norwegian Rats Are Smarter

*M*ost of the NYPD station houses were built many years ago. They're being modernized now, but they are in bad shape. It's even hard to take a nap in a station house lounge because rats or mice or bedbugs run across your legs—it's disgusting. They used to have exterminators come in, and one of them sat down with us and talked about the rats in New York. He says, "You got American rats and Norwegian rats. The American has a kind of rounded snout while the Norwegian has a longer snout. Both are very smart and difficult to catch."

"Well," one cop asked, "which is smarter?"

"The Norwegian," the exterminator said. "He found his way here from Norway, didn't he?"

MAY I STORE YOUR ILLEGAL GUN IN A SAFE PLACE, SIR?

Cops today are getting pushed more and more to be politically correct. The only problem is the perps don't have a set of rules. So they can make bogus complaint after bogus complaint and nothing will happen to them, but the officer has to go through all kinds of stuff to defend himself. One cop got so fed up, he made up a questionnaire for perps, whom he refers to as "customers." Some cops actually hand them out, and some customers are so dense that they fill in the form:

NEW PRISONER
SURVEY FORM FOR NYPD
CUSTOMER SURVEY FORM
2005-UP-YOURZ

All customers (formerly called prisoners) of the NYPD are to be given this form and a pen. It should be collected before prisoner, er—customer, is transported to CB [Central Booking]. Failure to give this form out will result in severe discipline to PO. A copy of this form is to be faxed to CCRB [Civilian Complaint Review Board] to see if a complaint will be filed against the PO. Form is to be faxed to CCRB BEFORE fingerprinting perp, er—customer.

TO THE CUSTOMER

Please fill this form out as accurately as possible. We are the new NYPD, and we are trying to adjust to the needs of you. After all, without you people, we'd be out of a job! If more than three questions are answered "no," a copy of this form is automatically sent to CCRB, and a complaint filed against the PO as a courtesy to you.

THE ARREST

- At what time were you arrested?
- What were you charged with?
- What do you think you should have been charged with?
- If you feel you should be let go IMMEDIATELY, please speak to the Desk Officer in precinct, even before giving him your pedigree. Sometimes the DO is hard of hearing. Speak LOUDLY; it's what they want.
- At any time did your PO dis your "colors," do-rag, or your gang tattoos?
- Did the PO use the fur-lined, soft velour, or NERF handcuffs?
- If you had a weapon of some sort in your hand and the PO shot at you after numerous requests for you to "drop the weapon," did the PO shoot you in the hand with the weapon in it?
- Did your PO call you sir/ma'am? If your PO called you ma'am, are you of the female sex?
- Were you transported to the precinct in an RMP [radio monitored patrol car]?
- Was the A/C working properly in the back of the RMP?
- Was there enough leg room, or did you have to sit sideways?

- Did the PO play your "music" on the radio? And at an excessive volume? Did your PO "crank the bass" till passersby's fillings were jarred loose? Did your PO tune in to Rush Limbaugh or some other talk show?
- Did your PO offer you a cool drink or offer to stop by Mickey D's for the dollar menu special?

IN THE HOUSE

- Did the desk officer greet you and welcome you to the precinct? Did he seem sincere in his greeting?
- Were you brought to a small private room away from everyone to be "tossed"?
- If answer to above question is no, and you had to stand in front of the desk, did the DO offer you a chair?
- What about offering you a cool drink or your favorite beverage from the machine?
- Were the cells clean and graffiti free?
- Were the cells at a comfortable temperature? Was the A/C working properly?
- Did your PO offer to get you a sweater if you were too cold?
- Was there plenty of seating space?
- Were the toilet facilities in the cell area working

and in a clean and presentable manner?

- Was there a pleasant smell or/and an air freshener in the toilet facility?
- Was there enough toilet paper and/or sanitary napkins available?
- If no, did the cell attendant get some in a reasonable amount of time?
- Were the periodicals in the toilet current and was there a new copy of the *New York Times*?
- Was the crossword already done?
- Were you arrested weekdays between two and five P.M., when each and every precinct has a free food buffet?
- Were the only sandwiches that were available tuna and it was only 2:15?
- Did all the chocolates have little holes in them from people "peeking" as to what they are?

FINGERPRINTING

- Did your PO make the fingerprinting process a memorable one?
- Did your PO explain why it takes forever for your prints to come back?
- Did your PO explain only peddler arrestees—er customers—are DAT eligible?

GENERAL QUESTIONS

- How often are you arrested? A month? A week?
- How would you compare this arrest to previous arrests? Would you want to be arrested by this officer again?
  If not, explain.
- Would you recommend to your customer friends and/or family to be arrested by this officer?
- Would you want to be arrested in this precinct again?
  If no, explain.

Thank you for participating in this survey. Your CCRB has been filed and an investigator will contact you sometime while you are in CB as to what you think the punishment should be for your PO. Once again thank you for choosing NYPD as your police department to be arrested with. We're trying harder to please you. Feel free to add your comments below.

THE HUNTER

☆

I had a sergeant named Richards. He was a great cop with about seventy gun collars, but he also thought of himself as a big hunter. He'd take all his time off to hunt, and without fail he'd come back with nothing. He always had an excuse. He'd say a deer was too small, or he didn't have a permit for a particular type of game. One day Richards calls five of us to a squad meeting in a back room, but we don't go all the way in because there's a bird in there. It's flying around, panicked, whacking against the window. Then it starts dive bombing at us, and one of the cops yells, "Get the pepper spray! Get the pepper spray!"

Another guy takes out his gun and says, "I'll shoot him."

Richards says, "Shut off the lights. He'll go away."

"Hey," says another cop. "It's a bird, not a moth! No wonder you never catch anything!"

A REAL COOL DUDE

Sometimes when you have an injury, the department puts you on desk duty or something like that until you heal and get back on the street. I hurt my hand and my neck, so I was on the T/S [telephone switchboard] for a while. Basically, you are in the front part of the station house just answering phones and directing people who come in off the street. It was pretty busy, so I decided to eat my veal parmigiana hero while I was answering the phones. It was hot and muggy, and we just got the air conditioning working in the station house. Some of these station houses are so old and run down that the heat doesn't get fixed until March, and they fix the A/C when summer is almost over. Anyway, this old homeless guy walks past the station house as someone is walking out. He feels the cool air hit him and decides to come in. He comes over to the T/S, leans on it, looking very tired, and says as he wipes the sweat from his forehead, "Man, da big apple is like da baked apple today."

"Yeah. It's a hot one, no doubt about it."

"Mind if I just rest here in the cool air, it is so hot outside?"

"Nah, go ahead."

Like I said, it was busy, and the T/S is lit up like a Christmas tree. So I am answering calls and transferring them to the right people for a couple of minutes, and the guy is still standing there. He looks at my half-eaten sandwich and says, "Mmmm mmmm, I'm starvin' like Marvin and dat looks good. What is dat, chicken parma-johnny?"

"No, veal. Do me a favor, pal. Go sit on the benches over there and get cool. It is too busy to be standing over me."

"Okay, no problem."

I turn my head for a second—I mean an instant—to tell another officer he has a phone call. The homeless guy reaches over with his filthy hands, picks up my sandwich, and asks, "You gonna finish dis half?"

I just look at him in amazement and yell, "Well, I'm not now." I kicked him out, but I let him keep it. I figured he needed it more than I did.

WHO
ARE YOU THEN?

☆

Working in South Central, you see and hear it all. A lot of the gang bangers are tough, but you can tell when you get a guy who is just acting tough and trying to fit in because he panics when it hits the fan. We were wurkIng a day tour when we get a call about a robbery. Some lady got robbed walking away from an ATM. So we get the victim, and another unit grabs the perp and holds him there for a showup. We pull up, and the victim says he's the guy who robbed her. I get out and tell the other sector guy, "Cuff him up, that's the guy!"

The perp panics and yells, "I ain't mc!"

GIVE A MAN ENOUGH ROPE . . .

It's no secret that cops and defense attorneys are not exactly bosom buddies. The lawyer's job is to make a testifying cop look bad. If they can do that then they have a great chance of getting their client off, so they are always trying to trip you up. However, since they are not exactly representing brain surgeons, it can backfire. I was in court on a robbery collar, and the lawyer for this mutt starts in on me and asks, "Officer Santana, did you give him Miranda?" (You know, the whole spiel about the right-to-remain-silent jazz you see on *Law and Order*.)

I respond, "Yes. In the patrol car."

The mutt jumps up from the defense table and starts yelling, "That's B.S.! He didn't give me any rights. That [bleeper] is lying."

The judge tells him to sit down and be quiet, that outbursts like that will not be tolerated. Things calm down a little, and then the defense attorney asks where I recovered the money and the gun from. I respond that the gun was in his left pants pocket and the money in his right pants pocket. Mutt jumps back up and yells, "This time he's telling the truth!"

Thank you, jackass. End of trial.

POLICE LINE – DO NOT POLICE LINE – DO N

What?

I think the trouble with a lot of the kids today is that they pick really bad role models. These four white kids dressed like gang members come boppin' into the precinct one night about two A.M. reeking of alcohol. They just came from an Eminem concert. The conversation was as follows:

Officer: "Can I help you?"

    Kid: "Myz car gots compunded."

Officer: "Why did your car get compounded?"

    Kid: "'Cause yo, myz license was provoked."

Officer: "Do you mean your car was impounded because your license is revoked?"

    Kid: "Dats what I've been tryin to say, offisah. Your cranium ain't listening to your clavicle."

HUH?

In the police academy they should definitely have a course on street lingo. Either that, or I have to start watching more MTV because I don't know what the heck the people are saying out there. I only had about eight months on the job when I had this conversation. It was a hot night, and we get a call about a fight in the middle of the street. We were the first unit to respond, and I ask these five kids hanging out what I thought was a simple question, "What happened?"

"Well, what had happen was he came out and was like *bap*. So she was like *oh word*? and then she said *boom*."

I am standing there thinking how do I put that in a report? I was looking for help with the translation from my partner or the other kids. My partner had about eight years on, and he was used to this. He understood everything and asks back, "So then what happened?"

"Yo, I don't know. I was just chillin' and everyone broke out."

NOT QUITE DOA

We get a call to an apartment in the projects. A nurse's aide has not been able to get into a patient's apartment for days and didn't have a key. So I pound on the door with my stick for a while and get no answer. I am thinking there's obviously a DOA inside. I call housing maintenance, and they drill the lock. The door swings open, and they all back off thinking, "Let the cop go in." Great, I love finding DOAs (not!). I walk in slowly, and look in the kitchen. There's food in the pan, and it's very old. I start to search the place and walk toward the bedroom. Sure enough, I see someone in the bed facing away, and I am thinking definitely a DOA. So, like a good cop, I want to get an idea of how long she was there. I lean over the bed to see her face, and she spins her head and yells, "What are you looking at!" I jumped back and nearly fell into her dresser. I was shot for the rest of the day.

Turned out she had been hearing voices for days and didn't want to answer the door. The EMTs carted her away to the psych ward.

Careful What You Wish For

*O*ne summer I was working the night tour, and they made us drive a civilian reporter around. She was taking summer courses at UMass to complete her senior year and was a journalism major. She was doing a story on relations between the police department and the community for her school newspaper. I had no problem with it because I have kids of my own, and I am always trying to help them further their education. If they want a glimpse of what we do and what we face, fine by me. As soon as she gets in the car she starts spouting off. "Oh, you guys don't really do much, I guess. Is it this slow every night? Why don't you look for some crime? Isn't it a waste to just cruise around here?"

I say to her, "Look, obviously when we ride with civilians we are not going to endanger their safety and bring them to anything too heavy where they can get hurt."

She took offense at this because she was this snotty, cop-hating, rich daddy's girl with major attitude. "Well I didn't lead a sheltered life, you know. I am a journalist and I can handle anything you guys run into!"

Five minutes later, we get a radio run to an old welfare hotel in a seedy part of the city. A skell must have paid a whole month's rent up front, then died the next day. About three weeks later, the smell is unbearable, and they call the police. The guy was dead for over two weeks. It had bloated, then burst, and he was being eaten by maggots. We tell the kid not to go in the room, it's too gruesome. Ms. Reporter starts with her feminist B.S. routine, so we tell her to go ahead and take a look. In less than three seconds, she projectile-vomited across the room, hitting the wall, then screamed and ran down the stairs to the patrol car. As she is running out, my partner yells out, "While we're finishing up here, think about where you want to eat dinner!"

YOU'LL KNOW 'EM
WHEN YOU SEE HIM

I work in a pretty normal suburban town—you know, houses with tree-lined streets, young families, that sort of stuff. I am doing a day tour when a call comes over about an escaped ostrich. I've seen a lot, and I know this is the suburbs—not exactly wild ostrich country. So like any normal cop would do, I pick up my radio and say, "What was that, did you say ostrich?"

The answer is yes, so I go to the complainant's house, and sure enough, the guy tells me he is a handler at a petting zoo but sometimes, to get the animals tame, he has them at his house in the yard. He designed his yard to house these animals but never had an ostrich there before. I have no idea if it is even legal to have an ostrich, but I figure I can come back to that later. Now I have to find this huge bird. So I put the guy in my car, and I get on the radio. "Be advised we have an escaped ostrich running around. If you find him, advise me of your location. I have the handler here with me."

Of course, everyone is getting a kick out of this except one guy, Schmidt, who is strictly by the book—an attitude that is sometimes grating. So he says: "Do you have a description of the ostrich?"

I can't let it go. "Where do you think we are, the Australian outback? Tell ya what, you come across any six-foot bird running down the street, and he'll do."

A Nasty Trick

I was with another rookie named Johnston, and we were left at the scene of a DOA to await the ME and the meat wagon. The DOA, who looked like he died of natural causes, was on the floor between the bed and the wall. Johnston was a former worker at the morgue and knew most of the MEs. He recognized the responding MEs name and decided he is going to play a joke on him. So he takes his shirt off, rubs talcum powder on his face and upper body, and gets into the bed and pulls the covers over himself. A short while later, the ME comes in and asks where the body is. I direct him to the bedroom. He starts asking questions I can't answer about medications and stuff, then pulls the blanket back, leans over, and starts to inspect the body. Johnston reaches up with both hands and grabs his throat. The ME fainted! I thought my career was toast. Thank the almighty that when he came to he remembered nothing! We just told him, "Must have been something you ate, Doc."

DO YOU KNOW WHO I AM? SURE . . .

Chicago has been mobbed up dating back to the Al Capone days. It's different from New York, where they have five families dividing up territories. Here it is just one family that controls everything. When Michael Jordan was playing for the Bulls, basketball was the big ticket, and everybody who was somebody wanted to go. So one night after a Bulls playoff game, all these limos were lined up outside waiting for their turn to leave. This one limo decides it is not going to wait and pulls a dangerous U-turn. Everyone is honking and yelling. I pull the guy over, and for safety reasons, my partner goes to the rear passenger side and makes them roll down their tinted windows. The driver starts to plead with me kind of nervous like, "Please don't give me ticket—my passenger told me to do it." The passenger can't hear him because there's a window between the front and the back.

I say, "Your passenger told you? Well, unless you have the president back there, I don't care what your passenger told you to do."

Then I hear my partner arguing with the passenger, and I tell the limo driver to roll down the dividing window so I can see what's going on. Turns out it is the well-known daughter of a top-echelon mobster who has been locked up for about five years, but the daughter is famous and making a living off his name. She has had a little to drink and is getting real annoyed when she finally screams out, "I'll have your badge! Do you clowns know who I am?" I say, "Yeah—an inmate's daughter."

ONLY IN NEW YORK

We were working a midnight tour when we get a call
to check out an aided case on a subway platform.
We show up, and the place is pretty deserted except
for one homeless guy passed out on the bench. We
go over and check him out, and he is DOA, natural
causes. New York in the summer can be hot, but in
the subway it's like a kiln. We were already dripping
sweat. Since we had to wait for the ME to certify the
guy was dead—something that could take hours—it
was going to be bad. So we chose another route. We
carried the guy's body onto the next train, propped
it up on a seat, and put a newspaper in his hands as
if he were a drunk sleeping it off. The train pulled
out of the station, and we went back on patrol.

A few hours later, we get contacted by Central
that there's an aided case but this time it is on the
train, not the platform. We enter the train, and see it
is the same guy just as we left him. He is still sitting
up, but without the paper. The guy who called to tell
us he was dead stole his paper. Only in New York.

JUST BEING
HELPFUL

We get a call about a robbery on Boone Street with a description of the perp. We see him on the street, and he starts to run. We catch up to him and start to put on the cuffs, but he looks at us in total bewilderment. "Hey," he says, "whatcha duin'? Whatcha doin'? What's going on?"

"You robbed a lady back there."

"I didn't rob no lady! I didn't rob no lady."

"Then why you running from us?"

"I was running after the guy who did it! I was trying to help you catch him! Come on, follow me before he gets away!"

POLICE LINE - DO NOT   POLICE LINE - DO N

True Love

We get a call about a domestic dispute in an older part of the city, and we go to the apartment, and find an elderly couple in their seventies. The woman says to us, "He's got the devil inside him. The devil inside him. He's drinking the devil's beverage."

So I ask, "What happened?"

"He's crazy. He's accusing me of cheating on him."

We go into the kitchen and the man is sitting at the table as calm as can be. He's drinking from a bottle of Scotch, and there's also a long machete that he must have gotten from the war. So we sit down and ask him, "What's the problem?"

"She's cheating on me. I know it. Every Wednesday night she goes out—"

The woman interrupts, "I ain't cheating on him. I go play bingo at the church!"

Then the couple starts arguing back and forth like cats and dogs about whether this is true, and my partner interrupts, "Listen, how long you guys been together?"

166

"Thirty-eight years," the man says.

So I say to him, "You think she's cheating on you after all these years? You really want to ruin your marriage now?"

The man looked shocked. "Married?" he says. "Married? I ain't married to that crazy woman! We just been sleeping together!"

LOOKS ARE IN THE EYE
OF THE BEHOLDER

One of the fun things about being a cop is the camaraderie and banter that goes back and forth between the guys. It is one constant chop-busting contest day in and day out.

I worked with one guy named Fast Eddie in the 109. He was a good cop and great friend of mine. On the side, he was also a very successful model, and the women all loved him. Because of it, he was an obvious target for everyday chop busting from the rest of the command, but he gave it back just as quick.

One day after our tour, we are all in the locker room changing to go home, and Fast Eddie was paying extra special attention to his appearance in the mirror. One of the old timers, a cop named Doyle, walks by and says, "Ya know, you spend more time in the mirror gettin' ready than my old lady."

Without taking his eyes off his reflection, Eddie says, "That's 'cause I'm better lookin' than your old lady."

WELL, YOUR HONOR, THIS IS WHAT HAPPENED . . .

Some stories are so unbelievable they're believable. Me and my partner are on patrol, and we see this car in front of us stopping, going, and weaving. We look though the rear window of the car, but we can't see a head or any indication that someone is driving. We pull the car over, and I go up to talk to the driver. When I get there, I find a very small Asian woman behind the wheel, and on her head is a shih tzu dog —right on her head! The dog's head is facing the back of the car, and his tail is in front of her face, going like a windshield wiper. She says, "Sorry. Dog jump around car. Jump on head."

I am looking at her in total disbelief, and I start telling her how she can barely see over the dashboard as it is. I am in total shock, so I tell her, "Keep the dog off your head and go." Then I go back to my partner, and he says, "You're not going to write her?"

"No. How can I? Where on the summons does it say 'Dog on head'? How would I explain this to a judge? He'll never believe me."

Cinderella

*T*he kids in the inner city used to wear their pants down over their butts with Timberland boots. The boots were always untied—it was the style. There was one guy wanted for a robbery, and a cop we worked with named Burns spotted him. The guy was big and muscled up, and he decided not to go peacefully. He wrestled with Burns, who was doing the best he could, but couldn't cuff him. Then another cop comes up and grabs the guy by the legs. His pants start to come down and one of the Timberlands comes off, but he gets away.

So Burns and the other officer radio in a description, including that he has one shoe on and one shoe off. After a couple of minutes, Central comes back and says, "Can you advise what size shoe it is?"

Burns says, "Never mind! Just bring Cinderella back to the ball!"

GLAD I COULD CHEER YOU UP

My partner and I went to the academy together and ended up working in the same precinct. One day we get a call about a jumper and we get there before ESU. When we arrive, we ask the neighbors what's going on. They say the guy is really distraught. His wife left him and took the kids, and he lost his job. He's in debt, and his mother just passed away. This guy's got a laundry list of troubles.

We go up to the roof, and the guy's pretty close to the edge. So my partner starts talking to him saying, "What's going on?"

"Everything is falling apart."

"Yeah, I know, your neighbors told me your wife left you, you lost your kids, you lost your job, you're in debt up to your eyeballs, your mother—"

"Hey," the guy says, interrupting, "If this is a pep talk, get to the peppy part!"

BEST DATE EVER

The department says it doesn't have a ticket quota, but it does. Unless you're on a special detail they expect you to write a book a month, which is twenty-five tickets. There were two guys who didn't meet their quota one month and then again the next month. They were punished pretty severely by having their sector car taken away for a month, and it was the summer. They had to walk a foot post rather that ride around in a nice air-conditioned car.

Then this duo was on a four-to-twelve tour shortly after they had their car taken away. They're walking around, and one says to the other, "Let's get some lunch."

They go to a nice sit-down lunch, and they're not worrying about missing something because they have their radios with them. The lunch lasts two hours, and then one says to the other, "What do you want to do now?"

"Let's go to a movie."

In the theater, one of the guys stays in the back

row for a half hour and puts the radio on low. Then he switches with his partner, and then back again. They do that until the movie is over. They leave the theater and again comes the question, "What do you want to do now?"

"Let's go over to the firehouse."

"Good. The Rangers game is on."

They go to the firehouse, take off their gun belts and shirts, and just relax and watch the game. Of course, the firemen love to cook, so one of them bakes brownies. While they're munching fresh brownies, one of the cops looks at a clock and says, "Hey, it's getting late. We better get back."

They put on their shirts and gunbelts, and while they're doing this, one of the cops looks over at the other, smiles warmly, and says, "You know what? This is the best date I've ever been on!"

Why Shotgun Teams Were Disbanded

*B*ack in the '60s, New York would sometimes put cops in what they call shotgun teams in locations where robberies were common to provide an unpleasant surprise for robbers. They would get the drop on the bad guys, and an arrest would follow. Shotgun teams were disbanded as the result of one team's actions. They hid behind a vent and waited for someone to come and rob a liquor store that had been held up five or six times earlier.

What happened was recounted by the perp who had been shot by the team and who was in a hospital. "I came into the joint," he says, "and put the heat on the dude. I tell him to give me all the bread in the register. As he's doing that, I hear a little noise to my right, and then I hear someone yell though I can't see anyone, 'Goodbye, [bleeper]!' And the next thing I know I wake up here."

FUNNY COP LINGO

Airmail. Concrete, bricks, and other items hurled down from rooftops onto patrol cars responding to a call.

Bag Bride. A prostitute who smokes crack cocaine.

Bernie. In the New York area, a potential crime victim who may look like easy prey to criminals but is emphatically not. "Bernie" refers to Bernhard Goetz, a mild-looking bespectacled man who was approached on a subway train by four youths—three brandishing sharpened screwdrivers—who asked for cigarettes and money. Goetz, who had been mugged twice before, reached into his pocket, produced a nine-millimeter automatic, and shot all four.

Blue Flu. Illness feigned by a group of police officers.

Boneyard. Also referred to as a bone orchard—the cemetery.

Bridge of Sighs. The nickname for an enclosed walkway between the courthouse and the old city prison in Manhattan called the Tombs.

Chalk Fairy. Outlining a corpse on the ground with chalk is standard procedure in a homicide investigation. Chalk outlines show not only where a body was located but also serve as markers that indicate where small bits of evidence like bullet casings and blood are located.

Chalking must only be done after the crime scene photographs are taken; otherwise, says Vernon J. Geberth in *Practical Homicide Investigation*, the defense attorneys can maintain that the crime scene has been contaminated. One photo in one of his books is captioned: "Here you see the deceased lying in the position in which he was found. The crime scene photo may possibly be 'inadmissible.' While the first officers were securing the scene, a 'chalk fairy' suddenly had the irresistible impulse to draw chalk lines around the body."

Death Fart. Gas expelled by a dead person.

Felony Flyers. Sneakers on a young inner-city male.

Grasseater. Police officer who takes small, insignificant bribes.

Ivory Tower. In New York City, One Police Plaza, police headquarters.

Jewish Lightning. Arson for profit.

Keister Stash. Illegal objects secreted in the rectum; also called a keister stow.

Lush Worker. Someone who steals from sleeping riders on subway trains.

GOYAKOD. Acronym, a reminder for homicide cops on how to conduct a murder investigation. Namely, "Get Off Your Ass and Knock On Doors!"

Meateater. A police officer who takes cash bribes.

Token Sucker. A thief who steals tokens from subway token machines by sucking them out. Before the New York city subway system switched to the MetroCard, subway riders used metal tokens. Though token suckers have vanished from the scene, they once were a force to be reckoned with in the city. They would jam paper into the slot where the tokens were deposited. Then, while the patron went back to the token seller to complain that the stile would not open, or perhaps simply went through a different turnstile, the token sucker would press his lips over the slot and suck the token out.

Trolling for Blues. Police officer dressing up as a potential victim and inviting attack.

This is a practice in PDs everywhere. It is frequently used where muggings or rapes are common. Both male and female officers troll; sometimes male officers dress as females. One candidate for the all-time record in trolling for blues is Bo Dietl, now a private investigator, who in his years on the job posed as a victim more than five hundred times.

Whore's Bath. Washing the armpits only, or any other cursory bathing.

Wood Shampoo. When multiple cops hit a perp's head with multiple blows of their batons.

Scott Baker, ex-New York city policeman and current owner of The Last Laff Comedy Club in Centereach, New York.

FUNNY COP STORIES
WANTED!

We hope you enjoyed reading these stories and some of them made you laugh, as one cop said, like a hyena. We need more for our second book. We welcome any from cops and civilians—just whatever made you laugh about cops' lives. You can send them to us by visiting us on the Web at www .funniestcopstories.com.

THANKS! STAY SAFE AND, IF YOU ARE A COP, SANE.